At the age of twelve, David Gr[...]
when the offering pan was pas[...]
a forecast for the rest of his life: he got up, stood on the offering pan, and gave himself. David's life story, *Born to Give*, will mesmerize you, challenge you, motivate you, inspire you, and bless you! It's a must-read!

—GEORGE O. WOOD
CHAIRMAN, WORLD ASSEMBLIES
OF GOD FELLOWSHIP;
GENERAL SUPERINTENDENT, THE GENERAL COUNCIL
OF THE ASSEMBLIES OF GOD, 2007–2017

The life of David Grant tells the story of how when someone surrenders fully to the purposes of God, He can use that person beyond imagination. As you read about how David's life has exceeded his dreams, I am confident you will be inspired to live out your calling in full surrender.

—DOUG CLAY
GENERAL SUPERINTENDENT, THE GENERAL COUNCIL
OF THE ASSEMBLIES OF GOD

After having read David Grant's story, in which he states that he never received a call to missions, I am certain that he had an encounter with the God of heaven. That encounter resulted in scores of people being saved, baptized in the Holy Spirit, and healed and many being called into full-time Christian ministry. To God be the glory!

—THOMAS E. TRASK
GENERAL SUPERINTENDENT, THE GENERAL COUNCIL
OF THE ASSEMBLIES OF GOD, 1993–2007

I thought I had heard all about the life of David Grant, having known him for years as a dear friend. I have laughed and cried with him as he has captivated audiences with stories about burying cats, baptizing chickens, and revealing his heart for the lost and suffering, especially those in India. But I was wrong. *Born to Give* will entertain you with exciting, heartfelt stories, but it will also challenge you to stretch beyond any preconceived capacity you thought you possessed—giving more than you thought possible.

—REV. ALTON GARRISON
DIRECTOR, ACTS 2 JOURNEY INITIATIVE;
ASSISTANT GENERAL SUPERINTENDENT, THE
GENERAL COUNCIL OF THE ASSEMBLIES OF GOD,
2007–2019

David Grant is a longtime personal friend. Through the decades, his life and ministry have reached millions of people around the world. This book will inspire, encourage, and challenge you to give your all for the work of the kingdom of God.

—GREG MUNDIS, DMIN
EXECUTIVE DIRECTOR, ASSEMBLIES
OF GOD WORLD MISSIONS

The world is desperate for heroes. Fortunately, I've had the privilege of knowing two of them—David and Beth Grant. They have demonstrated what it means to go beyond occasional acts of compassion to selfless living. As a result, thousands of women and girls have been rescued and given a future through Project Rescue. *Born to Give* is the compelling story of how

David Grant became the person he is—a selfless hero who has left an imprint on my life and many others'. I am grateful this book was finally written.

—HAL DONALDSON
PRESIDENT, CONVOY OF HOPE

Giving! Missions! That really describes David Grant. Even his wife and children embody these same attributes and more. Having known David for over fifty years and shared ministry in different ways, I can tell you that this book *is* David Grant. Every word is his voice speaking to you, as if you were sitting together over coffee. Yet his deep conviction and passion will stir your heart to love, serve, and give it all to Jesus.

This book is a must for young people and Bible college students. Buy it, read it, and live it. It will change a generation.

—NAOMI DOWDY
FOUNDER, TCA COLLEGE, SINGAPORE;
FORMER SENIOR PASTOR, TRINITY CHRISTIAN
CENTRE, SINGAPORE

David Grant is truly a missionary legend! If you have heard him speak in person, you will relive that experience while reading *Born to Give*. If not, you are in for a new experience and special blessing. David genuinely lives what he writes and preaches, and God has used him to inspire hundreds of thousands to experience greater blessings through the gift of generosity.

—RANDY HURST
SPECIAL CONSULTANT TO THE EXECUTIVE DIRECTOR,
ASSEMBLIES OF GOD WORLD MISSIONS

I've had the privilege of hearing my friend David Grant preach many times. Reading his book *Born to Give* opens a fresh and wonderful door to look inside at the path of his life, feeling his story, laughing, crying, and being moved by his spiritual passion. I love this book!

What I've learned over the years is that when a person's life and story are in fact backed up by genuine action and longtime faithfulness of staying true to his or her calling, that's something to celebrate. And I celebrate David Grant for being the kind of person who embodies the best of us!

David tells the story of the preacher who had cast a compelling vision of God's provision and was challenged later by a listener: "What if God does not come through with those provisions you talk about?" The reply was profoundly simple: "What if He does?" David has lived a life of positive faith, believing and preaching the "What if He does?" part of being a Christ follower!

—T. RAY RACHELS
SUPERINTENDENT, SOUTHERN CALIFORNIA DISTRICT
COUNCIL OF THE ASSEMBLIES OF GOD, 1988–2010;
EXECUTIVE PRESBYTER, THE GENERAL COUNCIL OF
THE ASSEMBLIES OF GOD, 2011–2021

It was a *command* from Jesus, not a suggestion: "And he said unto them, Go ye into all the world, and preach the gospel to every creature" (Mark 16:15, KJV). My friend David Grant has spent his life obeying that directive. In virtually every area of ministry, especially across India, Grant's preaching, teaching, giving, and lifestyle have made a huge footprint. In recent years he has even been imprisoned for delivering Christ's message in places it was not wanted because it was not known. The judgment seat of Christ (1 Cor. 3:10–13) will reveal the impact of the obedience of David and his faithful wife, Dr. Beth Grant, to the commission from our Lord.

The book you hold in your hand has the potential to radically change the way you think about missions and what it really means to follow Jesus. A copy of it should be in every home—and read!

—DAN BETZER
FORMER HOST, *REVIVALTIME* BROADCAST;
SPEAKER; PASTOR

It has been said that every life is a story. That is true. Some of the stories are bad, some are good, and a few are great. The story of David Grant is a great one. From humble beginnings as the son of an itinerant Pentecostal pastor to becoming one of the most effective missionary evangelists of his generation, a single core value has guided his story to greatness. David lives to give. He gave his youth. He gives his earnings. He gave his personal comfort and delayed thoughts of marriage until the age of thirty. He gives himself to God and missions. *Born to Give* is his story. It unfolds from a little boy who gave God his life in an offering plate to a man touching the world. His beloved India is a better place today because of his giving. Millions of dollars has been raised, tens of thousands of souls are saved, and thousands of abused lives are redeemed because he never stops giving. Now he gives his great story, and many of the small ones, to us. The gift is magnificent. It calls us to *be* more, *do* more, *give* more. This book should be required reading for every follower of Jesus. And the reading should guide our offerings to Him.

—TERRY RABURN,
SUPERINTENDENT, PENINSULAR FLORIDA DISTRICT
COUNCIL OF THE ASSEMBLIES OF GOD

Not only is David Grant my mentor and friend; he is also the most generous person I have ever known. There is no one I know more qualified to write on this subject.

—JOSEPH GORDON

Born
to Give

Born
to Give

David Grant

CHARISMA
HOUSE

Most Charisma House Book Group products are available at special quantity discounts for bulk purchase for sales promotions, premiums, fund-raising, and educational needs. For details, call us at (407) 333-0600 or visit our website at www.charismahouse.com.

Born to Give by David Grant
Published by Charisma House
Charisma Media/Charisma House Book Group
600 Rinehart Road, Lake Mary, Florida 32746

Unless otherwise noted, all Scripture quotations are taken from the Holy Bible, New International Version®, NIV®. Copyright © 1973, 1978, 1984, 2011 by Biblica, Inc.® Used by permission of Zondervan. All rights reserved worldwide. www.zondervan.com. The "NIV" and "New International Version" are trademarks registered in the United States Patent and Trademark Office by Biblica, Inc.®

Scripture quotations marked kjv are from the King James Version of the Bible.

Visit the author's website at www.projectrescue.com.

Cataloging-in-Publication Data is on file with the Library of Congress.

International Standard Book Number: 978-1-63641-085-2
E-book ISBN: 978-1-63641-086-9

The author has made every effort to provide accurate accounts of events, but he acknowledges that others may have different recollections of these events. Every effort also has been made to provide accurate internet addresses at the time of publication, but neither the publisher nor the author assumes any responsibility for errors or for changes that occur after publication. Further, the publisher does not have any control over and does not assume any responsibility for author or third-party websites or their content.

In 2001 Calcutta was renamed Kolkata, reflecting the Bengali pronunciation of the name. The author refers to the city as Calcutta throughout this book because it is a familiar, historical spelling and most of the events recounted occurred while the city was called Calcutta.

21 22 23 24 25 — 9 8 7 6 5 4 3 2 1
Printed in the United States of America

CONTENTS

PREFACE

UDIENCES AROUND THE world have heard me tell stories about my parents, baptizing chickens, burying cats. They have wept with me as I've recalled the horrors of little girls and boys being sex trafficked in Southern Asia, and we have rejoiced together as we celebrated the goodness of the God who rescues, redeems, and restores the "least of these."

Friends, family, and colleagues have encouraged me for years to put the stories into print. I resisted because it seemed to me the story was still being written. But when my ministry in India reached its fiftieth anniversary, I felt an urgency in my heart to tell the stories one more time that have blessed and challenged so many people. I also wanted to tell the stories behind the stories and to share my heart.

I told the audience at a Light for the Lost convention that I've preached two sermons thousands of times.

Even that is not quite accurate; I've preached one message thousands of times. It is the message of "Christ and Him crucified." It is the message of how His blood cleanses the heart, the mind, the memory, and even the blood of anyone, anywhere, who puts their faith in Him.

It's been said that Southerners speak a language that's a lot like English. That was truer of the South of my youth than it is today. Throughout this book I have retained the flavor and cadences of Southern English where I thought it could be understood by the reader. I've done the same with the language of the Pentecostal subculture in which I grew up. Words like *saved, the rapture, the second coming,* and *backsliding* were part and parcel of my upbringing. Updating some of these terms would not convey the meanings as forcefully.

As I finish sixty years of ministry, I know who I am and I know what I'm supposed to do. I believe I was born to give, born to share this life-changing message as a missionary and to take as many people with me as I can. I'm amazed at how God could take a little boy from Pensacola, Florida, and use him to touch the nations.

Chapter 1

THE MOST SAVED PERSON I KNOW

I AM THE MOST saved person I know. A preacher's kid, I'm sure I've been saved at least 150 times. No evangelist ever had an unsuccessful revival in my dad's church because I got saved every night. It didn't matter what the sermon was about, I went to the altar. I got saved so often that I wore my own path in the carpet.

Dad's favorite sermon was about the rapture. That's all he preached. I can still hear his raspy voice saying, "Jesus could come tonight at midnight, and nobody is going. For straight is the way and narrow is the gate, and nobody finds it. Two will be in the bed, and neither one is going to make it. Nobody's going!"

The only hope he gave us was, if you came to the altar right then, you might have a chance. So I went to

1

the altar, every night. Every night! The sermons were filled with guilt. If you had a bad thought, that was enough to keep you out of heaven—and you'd better come forward. I went to the altar every night because I had lots of bad thoughts—and not just thoughts; I had a bunch of bad actions.

If they couldn't get you with the rapture, they would get you with the unpardonable sin. I wasn't sure what the unpardonable sin was, but I knew I had committed it. I lived in guilt, absolute guilt. Every time something was wrong, I was guilty.

It seemed as if I was always in trouble. My brothers and I were part wolf pack and part tribe. We fought almost every day, and almost every day Dad gave us a whipping. Often my grandmother would intercede on my behalf, saying, "Curtis, he's just a boy."

My dad was ready with a reply: "He's a little boy but he's full of the devil, and I'm gonna get the devil out of him. We can pray him out or we'll beat him out, but I tell you, he will go."

Every boy should have a grandmother like mine. My grandmother could see no wrong in her grandson. I was the joy of her life. She gave us everything we wanted. Did you want a milkshake in the middle of the night? No problem. When challenged, she simply explained, "If that child dies tonight, you will always regret you didn't give him his last request." Dad's approach was, well, you know what it was. God is not your grandmother.

I can remember Teen Challenge groups coming to my dad's church. A preacher named David Wilkerson started Teen Challenge in the late 1950s as an outreach to street gangs and drug addicts in New York City. An Australian aborigine could not have been more exotic in the rural South of my youth than the guys from Teen Challenge. They shared fascinating stories about drugs, women, darkness, and demonism. It was as close as a Pentecostal kid could get to sin without having to repent. The Teen Challenge guys had something we church kids did not—a testimony.

A testimony conferred superstar status. No matter how violent, depraved, or dysfunctional you were, a hell-to-heaven testimony qualified you for ministry. Transfixed, the congregation leaned forward in rapt attention. There was nothing like having a testimony. It almost made you want to go out and sin so you could get a testimony. Whenever I was feeling apologetic about not having a sensational story of redemption, I felt as if God reminded me, "I haven't called you to talk about the pit. I called you to talk about My promises!"

But avoiding sin had its own problems because everything was a sin. My dad preached against everything. What could we do? Nothing! Where could we go? Nowhere! Everything was a sin, every place was a sin. Going to the movies was a sin; so were the bowling alley and roller-skating rink. And dancing? Dancing was at the top of the list. Rock-and-roll music came straight from the pit of hell. The only place we could go was to church, so we went to church, where we heard long sermons. It seemed that preachers went on forever. You felt like the tribulation was half over before they finished. We were there hour after hour. We didn't have nice, padded pews. We had those old pine-slab benches that would split and pinch you when you got up. Then one day I had a discovery. One of my buddies sat down beside me. When my chronic hyper-activity forced me to jump up, the board pinched him. From that day on, I made it my goal to sit in that same spot. I had discovered the cure for everlasting church services.

When my brothers and I were small, Mother would put a quilt under the pew to help us survive those long services. My two brothers and I would climb down off the pew and lie on the pallet. If you put three little boys together on a pallet, you can be certain there'll be trouble. My older brother would lean over and hit me in the eye, and then I would dig my teeth into his ear. My eye was hurting and his ear was bleeding, but not one sound came from underneath that pew. Lose an eye or lose an ear, but if Daddy heard one squeal, you would lose your life.

Dad preached against television. Television! He said it was like a commode sitting in your living room, flushing sewage into the minds of your children. So we had to go to the deacon's house to watch TV. Thank God for deacons with TVs.

Chapter 2

GROWING UP GRANT

I'VE TALKED A lot through the years about how strict Dad was. As kids we often got frustrated with him. Mother would reply, "If you knew where he came from, you would understand."

Dad's family were hardscrabble farmers in Holmes County, Florida, right on the Alabama state line. Folks from there call it "LA," Lower Alabama, and the description fits. It was as Southern, as rural, and as poor as you can get. They lived in the little community of Sweet Gum Head, which might sound a little strange, but "Sweet Gum" was the name of a spring at the head of a creek. In those days, the Florida Panhandle wasn't considered to be good for much, which led the Florida state legislature to offer to give the region to the state of Alabama. Alabama wouldn't take it.

Sometime around the start of the First World War,

Charlie Grant married Barbara Hudson. The marriage produced six children. The oldest son was Curtis, my father, born in 1919.

Charlie Grant's family came from Scotch-Irish settlers who landed in New York City in the mid-1800s and migrated south into Virginia and then to Alabama and Florida. It was a rough family. The Grants had a reputation for domestic violence and moonshining. This was back in the 1890s.

It wasn't just the men who were tough. My Aunt Pearlie was as tough as any man and could handle a shotgun. She married an alcoholic who would go out drinking and then come home and beat her. Pearlie got fed up and finally told him, "The next time you come home drunk, I'm going to kill you." One night he came up the path reeling drunk and cussing. She pulled out a shotgun and blew off both his legs. He spent the rest of his life in a wheelchair. After he recuperated, Aunt Pearlie took him to church, where he got saved, and they became a happy couple. He couldn't go out drinking anymore, and he certainly couldn't beat her up. So I think it's fair to say that Dad came out of a tough background.

The Hudsons were a godly family. Like a lot of the South's rural poor, they were Scotch-Irish but also a mix of Creek, Cherokee, and Choctaw. All three of these tribes could be found in Alabama and Georgia. Sometimes I'm Cherokee, sometimes I'm Choctaw, sometimes I'm Creek, depending on the situation.

When my sister Gloria applied to work at a federal nuclear plant, they said they were only hiring immigrants, "but if you're Native American, we can hire you." So Gloria told them her grandfather was Cherokee. She got the job.

Barbara Hudson was a woman of prayer and quite a lady. In a world of violence, she believed that God would save and care for all six of her children. We don't know much about Barbara, but we know she loved Jesus. My dad was not her first child; two girls preceded him. The first one died.

Dad grew up during the Great Depression of the 1930s, when a quarter of the nation's workforce was unemployed. It was worse in the South where the Depression started for farmers almost ten years sooner. They had no money and no way to make any except for bootlegging, which meant making and running moonshine. Lots of good folks had a moonshiner in the family.

Dad lost his mother when he was eleven and she was in her midtwenties. The fact is his mother's cause of death is unknown, but rumors persist. There is a very real possibility Barbara Hudson's death was related to domestic violence. A cruel man who slept with a gun under his pillow and threatened to shoot his second wife with it if she dared get out of line was certainly capable. His violence and temper were public knowledge. Domestic violence was as sickeningly familiar a reality then as it is now. But just before Barbara died, she called the eleven-year-old Curtis to her bedside and said, "God's gonna use you to lead this whole family to Jesus." I don't know if Dad understood what she was talking about, but he never forgot it.

Dad left home at the age of thirteen and went to work for another farmer, breaking horses. At fourteen, he went to work in a cotton mill in Geneva, Alabama, about fifteen miles from home. His older sister, Marie, already had a job there. Every Friday evening Charlie would show up, take Marie's and Dad's pay envelopes, and go back to Holmes County.

Dad moved around a lot. I'm sure that's where I got my restless spirit. When he was seventeen, he landed a job in Bonifay, Florida, the county seat of Holmes County. He started attending a "brush arbor" revival meeting. Going back to the early 1800s, churches throughout the rural South would construct brush arbors, shedlike structures made of branches on the top and open on the sides. All summer long the churches would have camp meetings—the evangelistic outreach—almost every night in the brush arbors. When I was a boy, I would often hear people talk about getting saved in a brush arbor.

Over a period of three months, Dad was saved, baptized in the Holy Spirit, and called to preach. My father, and millions of people like him, came out of the camp meeting culture. It shaped the way they understood God, salvation, worship, and even the way they thought. The brush arbors could be raucous, intensely emotional affairs where the "sinners"—meaning local rowdies, lapsed church members, and adolescents like Dad—connected with God. The brush arbor was like the Temple in ancient Israel. It was the place where heaven touched earth and where people were touched by heaven, often in highly dramatic encounters. Sinners wept and shook when they repented of their sins and shouted when they experienced a breakthrough. Many of them were never the same.

Today, most churches have no place for anything remotely like the brush arbors. Today's brand of evangelical religion has become a sedate and predictable affair that emphasizes the process of discipleship with none of the explosiveness of the brush arbor. I'm not a theologian, but I knew a lot of the moonshiners and drunks who came out of the brush arbors, and I can testify to the power of the gospel to save, heal, and deliver.

Dad went home at the end of the summer, visited his father, and told him about what had happened, including the call to preach. Charlie said, "I would rather see you dead than preaching." Curtis always said that his father then grabbed a two-by-four and drove him out of the house. It took a long time for my grandfather to come around. He got saved when he was seventy-two years old and lived to be ninety-nine.

Dad went back to the pastor and said, "What do I do now?"

The pastor said, "It's Wednesday night, we have a service, and you're preaching."

Dad was seventeen years old. Over the next five years, he traveled the same back roads to the same towns where I preached thirty years later. Dad's revivals brought him back to Columbus, Georgia.

It was in Columbus that Curtis met his wife, Bonnie, a beautiful, eighteen-year-old Christian girl out of East Highland Assembly of God. Mother grew up as one of seven children with an alcoholic father who was basically absent. The family was supported by my mother's four older brothers. My mother always had a heart for God and a deep desire to serve him. When she became a high-schooler, she felt called to the mission field, specifically to India. She wanted to go to a new Bible school in New Brockton, Alabama, that became Southeastern University in Lakeland, Florida, where I later attended. But her family said, "No, nice girls don't go off to Bible school." I don't believe her family really believed that; I think they just wanted her to stay home.

Bonnie graduated high school and went to work as a secretary. After a few months, a young evangelist named Curtis Grant came to town. He proposed marriage, and she thought, "Well, I think this would be acceptable," and married my father. Five children and fifteen years later, it was obvious to Bonnie that she was not going to the mission field, but she prayed, "God, give me one child that will go to India in my place."

My mother didn't tell me about this prayer until I

came home from India at the age of twenty-three. I went into the kitchen, picked her up off the floor, and said, "Momma, God's called me to India."

She said, "Put me down, boy. I knew it from the moment you were born."

My parents spent several months on the evangelistic field before taking their first church in Eufaula, Alabama. My mother almost died in Eufaula giving birth to their first son, Curtis Joel. The doctor didn't want to treat a Pentecostal woman. Pentecostals were not nearly as well accepted then as they are today. Our churches were usually located on "the other side of the tracks," in the poorest parts of town. The people attracted to them were from the bottom tier of Southern society. Many Baptists, Methodists, and Presbyterians saw them as odd at best and cultish at worst. They viewed Pentecostals with an air of suspicion and disdain.

Despite the doctor's criminal negligence, God preserved my mother's life. I often think of my mother's brush with death because of prejudice when I see the trouble that the poor women in India have getting medical care. I see them and see my mother's face.

After Eufaula, Dad and Mom served pastorates in Pensacola, Florida, and in the nearby towns of Holley, Bagdad, and Milton—places you've never heard of unless you've been there.

Then in 1945, while pastoring First Assembly of God in Milton, Florida, David Lowell Grant was born. Two years later, while pastoring Brent Assembly in Pensacola, Lemuel came along. Six years later, in Tallahassee, Gloria arrived. Tim was born during one of Dad's longer pastorates, in Greer, South Carolina, where he stayed for two years. When I was a boy, it seemed as if we were always moving. Dad was an evangelist at heart and perpetually restless. I think he ran revival meetings of twelve and eighteen months. He loved to move and loved new places. He had moved a lot when he was a boy. That sense of restlessness was built into our family, and it still shows itself to this day in Curtis' children.

The five of us have moved all over the world. We learned to carry our world with us. Wherever we went, we had our best friends with us. From the time I was born until he landed back in Pensacola in 1957, Dad pastored eleven churches.

Near the end of his pastoral ministry, Dad took a church in Birmingham, Alabama. When he interviewed with the church board, they told him they wanted to reach the lost. Dad took them at their word. People started getting saved. Within a few months the church had doubled in attendance. Dad encouraged the new believers to join the church. The board was having none of it. They refused to approve any of the new people for membership. Dad being Dad challenged the decision. The board members admitted they wanted the church to grow but didn't want new members. They were happy with the way things were, especially with their power.

All that said, Dad knew God and was a man of great faith. Throughout the 1940s and '50s, polio ravaged every city and town in the United States. Many of its victims spent the rest of their lives in wheelchairs or struggling to walk in heavy steel braces. Some children lived out their days in iron lungs. The worst cases died. Parents and children lived in terror of contracting the dreaded disease.

Once, when I was a baby, I became ill and within a few hours had a high fever and showed all the symptoms of polio. My parents rushed me to the hospital. The doctor told my parents they could not run any tests until Monday but they would admit me. Dad sprang into action: "We dedicated this baby from his birth to the Lord for the ministry. If you can't run any tests until Monday, I'm going to take him home and bring him back on Monday."

The next morning Dad and Mom took me to church and laid me on the altar. They invited the church to come lay hands on me and pray. The congregation gathered around me, and Dad lifted his hands and his voice, praying, "Lord, I have dedicated David to You and to Your service. I am laying him on this altar and asking You to heal him now."

My mom, Bonnie Grant, was a great pastor's wife, a wonderful mother, and a loving Maw Maw to her grandkids. She was so ready to go to heaven by the time she reached ninety that on the day of her homegoing, she told her doctor, "I'm going to heaven today! Don't slow me down!"

My dad, Curtis Grant, shown with my mom, Bonnie, and their three oldest children (from left): Joel, me, and Lemuel. Dad, shown below later in his life, was an evangelist at heart and perpetually restless, moving us a lot as he pastored churches throughout the South.

Me—"little David Lowell"—with my big brother, Joel, my number one protector

All five of us Grant kids—(from left) Tim, Gloria, Lem, me, and Joel—have moved all over the world, sharing the gospel.

The next morning when they took me back to the hospital, the fever was gone and the tests showed there was no polio in my body. For Dad, Jesus as Savior, Healer, Baptizer in the Holy Spirit, and soon-coming King wasn't just a doctrine, it was reality. Hebrews 13:8 declares, "Jesus Christ is the same yesterday and today and forever." Dad believed that—Jesus had not changed. Whatever happened to our family, and whatever needs we had, Dad was always sure Jesus would come through.

The three older Grant boys were constantly in trouble. Dad was strict. We got whipped almost every day. Now that I'm a safe distance from my father's whippings, I think I understand his motivation. I'm sure he was afraid that the same wild, violent, hard-living streak was alive in us that had been in him and his family, and he was determined to beat it out of us. From this distance, I think he and my mother did a pretty good job. All five of us are serving God today. Two of their children and eighteen of their grandchildren became ministers or missionaries. Not bad for a bootlegger's son.

In 1951 the Grant family moved to Lake Village, Arkansas, where I started school. Lake Village was a country town with a little church right near the Mississippi River. It was low-lying delta country, and when it rained the whole area was buried in mud. We had a two-bedroom parsonage where my two brothers and I slept in one bedroom, and Dad and Mom slept in the other.

Like many of the church folk, we had a horse, and we hunted on horseback. Dad owned a Tennessee Walker—a great horse that was smart and, for a family living on a pastor's salary, expensive. When the three of us boys were around him, he would stand absolutely still. When we were on him, he would walk very slowly. But when Dad put the saddle on him, he could barely get on the horse. He started dancing and prancing—ready to go. From the moment Dad put his foot in the stirrup, he was gone. Dad took a lot of pride in that horse and claimed he could lay his rifle down between its ears and shoot, and the horse would never flinch.

Dad supplemented his meager salary in Lake Village by driving a school bus. One day the school bus slid off the road into a ditch, so deep in the mud that two tractors couldn't pull it out. I don't remember how they got it out, but I remember how impressed we were that both of the tractors together couldn't get the job done.

A few months later, we moved back across the river to the little town of Columbia, Mississippi, where I attended second grade. We were there for a year and then moved to Tallahassee, Florida, where Dad pastored Oak City Assembly of God. That was third grade. We lived on a forty-acre farm at the edge of town. We had a horse and calves. Since there were three boys and only one horse, we would ride the calves. When

Dad was away preaching revivals, Joel would ride the horse into town to the post office and the store.

Dad started the church in Pensacola when I was eleven. There were no church planting teams in those days, no financial support from the denomination. We were on our own. Dad didn't receive much salary. People would sometimes give him a "Pentecostal hand-shake," which means they would shake his hand and slip a little offering into his palm. Others would invite us to their homes for Sunday dinner or give us vegetables out of their gardens.

I thought we were the richest people in all of Pensacola. We lived in a two-bedroom parsonage with one bathroom. We were a family of seven in the Pensacola years, but there were seldom just seven people in our house—usually a dozen because missionaries stayed with us all the time. Half my life was spent sleeping on the living room floor because a missionary was sleeping in my bed.

One of the best parts of my childhood was having missionaries stay in our home, sitting around the dining room table till midnight every Sunday night, hearing stories of Africa, India, China, and Latin America. We didn't have television; we had missionaries. We had missionaries almost every week. A missionary would come and start talking about kids who had never heard of Jesus, and that would get my dad every time. Dad always had a soft spot for kids. He would reach for his billfold, and I knew they were going to get every nickel we had, including our lunch money for next week. They not only got Dad's money, they got mine. When Dad pastored in western Maryland, the church gave one-half of its income to missions. That was my Dad's heart.

Every Sunday we'd ask, "What are we going to do?"

Dad would say, "Don't worry about it. We're going to take care of God's business, and God's going to take care of us." There were never limits to his giving. I want you to know that God did a wonderful job of taking care of us. Bags of groceries would appear almost every week. We never saw anyone bring them; they were just there. My mom and dad were pioneer pastors, and we fed an average of forty people a week in our house. Dad was one of those old-fashioned country preachers who would say to everyone who dropped by our house, "Y'all get out and come eat." My mother never cooked a meal, she cooked all the time—from morning until night. There were always beans on the stove, cornbread in the oven, and some sort of soup. I get hungry just thinking about it.

Dad's compassion was not limited to missionaries and foreign lands. He also had a great ministry to alcoholics. It was nothing for someone to knock on our door at midnight, hungry or under conviction, and Dad would invite them into the kitchen, lead them to the Lord, pray with them, and give them a meal. There was something about our house that drew people. They wanted to stay.

Chapter 3

LIFE IN AN OFFERING PLATE

P EOPLE OFTEN ASK me, "David, when were you called to preach?" I usually reply, "I don't know if I was ever called; I think I volunteered."

I can never remember not wanting to be a preacher. In those days, you would often hear preachers talk about how they ran from the call of God. They would say, "I ran and I ran, and finally God caught me. I didn't want to preach, and I didn't want to go to the mission field, but God made me." That was not me. From the time I was a child I said, "Jesus, I want to preach. Please let me go to the mission field." All my life, that's all I wanted to do.

I started early. When I was four or five years old, we would visit my grandmother in Columbus, Georgia, and while the adults were visiting inside, I had church outside. Other kids might re-fight the great battles of the Civil War or World War II, but I would gather my brothers and cousins and have church. We would have a song service and announcements, then I would preach. Of course, no service was complete without an altar call. My brothers and cousins were like me; they got saved hundreds of times.

All the neighborhood kids had church in our front yard. Our cat died, and we decided to have a funeral. We got a shoebox and put the cat in the box. We had to break his tail in three places to get all of him in the box. We had a wonderful funeral. I preached that cat right into heaven. It was so good we dug him up the next day and did it all over again. When we dug him up on the third day, Momma caught us. The cat was smelling by then, and Momma said, "Bury that cat and leave him in peace." We cried because we had heard a cat has nine lives.

Dad bought a bunch of chickens and put them in the backyard. Sunday night was a water baptismal service. On Monday my brother, who was always leading me astray, said, "David, those chickens aren't going to heaven; they haven't been baptized."

"I will baptize the chickens," I replied with an air of holy determination. We couldn't find any water, but Dad had a big can of gasoline right outside the house. When Dad came home, all the chickens were laid out dead. We baptized them in gasoline, and they all died.

He shouted, "Who killed the chickens?"

I said, "We didn't kill them. We baptized them in the name of the Father, the Son, and the Holy Ghost, and God took them to heaven."

This was my childhood—burying cats and baptizing chickens.

I grew up not just wanting to be a preacher; I had a fire inside of me to be a missionary. I think one reason was because so many missionaries stayed in our home. Those missionary story nights got in my blood. At midnight, the missionaries got our bed and Momma made a pallet for us boys on the living room floor. I can remember lying down on that pallet and soaking my pillow with tears, saying, "Jesus, please let me be a missionary. Let me go where nobody has ever gone with the good news of Jesus. Let me build churches where churches have never stood. Let me feed kids who are hungry. Let me go where there's demon possession and darkness, and where there are lepers and people who are hungry and dark. In the darkness, let me help many."

When I was twelve, the great pioneer missionary Charles Greenaway preached at my dad's church. He preached like it was a crowd of thousands. No one could preach a missions service like Charles Greenaway. If there are apostles today, Charles Greenaway was one of them. Charles and his wife, Mary, flew to Togo, West Africa, in 1944. There was not much there in those days. Charles took the gospel to hundreds of villages. He laid hands on the sick and cast out devils. He faced down witch doctors. Tens of thousands of people turned to God. When Charles Greenaway told those stories, you felt like you were there. You could feel the African sun beating down on your head. You could taste the dust in the back of your throat. You could see the tears streaming down the faces of a people steeped in darkness for centuries.

And you wanted to go.

He told the story of a twelve-year-old boy who had no money to put in the missionary offering. At the end of the service when they passed the offering pan, the boy laid it on the floor, stood up in it, and said, "God, I don't have any money, but You can have me."

I was so deeply moved by Brother Greenaway's story that when they passed the offering plate that night, I said, "God, if that boy can do it, so can I." When the offering pan came by, I laid it on the floor, stood up in it, and the Holy Spirit spoke to my twelve-year-old heart and said, "David, you will go to India." And from that moment until now, I've been on my way to India.

Not long after that, I made my first faith promise. Faith promises have been a staple of evangelical missions for more than two hundred years. A faith promise is not a pledge; it's an expression of faith that, as God helps you, you will give the amount God puts in your heart. I promised God $10 a week, every week—$520 a year as a twelve-year-old boy. I was making $20 a week from a part-time job, and I gave half of it to missions. When I was sixteen, I got my first full-time job.

They paid me $50 a week, and I gave half of that to missions—roughly $1,200 a year from a sixteen-year-old. Faith promises taught me that giving was not about what I could do for God, but what God could do through me.

It took a few more years after putting my life in the offering plate before I finally lost my fear about the rapture and my fear of failure—of never being good enough to serve God. I can't tell you when it happened, but one day I read the verse in Acts that says, "Whosoever shall call on the name of the Lord shall be saved" (Acts 2:21, KJV). And I said, "Lord, I have called on Your name, and You have answered. I'm not going to the altar again for salvation. I'll go to the altar for baptism of the Holy Spirit, healing, or commitment, but I'm not riding on this spiritual roller coaster anymore. I'm getting off. I am saved."

I nailed my fear of the rapture to the cross that day. I've had a lot of questions in the last sixty years but never again struggled with the question of my relationship with God. Once I got that settled, my course was set.

I started preaching at fifteen. At sixteen I was traveling throughout the South, and by the time I was seventeen, I was preaching five hundred times a year. I have preached more than twenty thousand sermons over the last fifty years. OK, for those of you who've heard me, maybe it would be more accurate to say that I've preached one sermon thousands of times.

I've traveled eight million miles and spent fifty years in India. I've had the joy of helping to plant over two thousand churches and build one hundred Bible colleges. Today more than five thousand young men and women have graduated from our Bible colleges in India. All because I decided to live my life in an offering plate. I never saw myself as a person of great talent. I never stood at the head of my class in school. I always believed the greatest ability I have, or anyone has, is availability.

As I said at the beginning of this chapter, I don't think I was called to preach; I volunteered. And I believe God looked down from heaven and saw a ten-year-old kid lying on a pallet in a parsonage floor in Pensacola, Florida, and said, "I'm going to send him to India."

Chapter 4

BROKEN BREAD

AFTER GRADUATING HIGH school, I preached revivals all over the state of Florida. I preached in little crossroad towns like Two Egg and Havana, Marianna and Apalachicola. I think I drove over every back road in the state. Sometimes I branched out and went to Alabama or Mississippi. Usually, I stayed with the pastor and his family. Sometimes I slept in the church. But it was great. I learned to pray, and I learned to preach. I learned how to minister to people.

I preached seven times a week. What I lacked in knowledge, I made up for with fervor. I preached so fast that people could hardly understand me. One lady told her pastor, "I don't understand a word that boy says, but I love the way he says it." I think that just about sums up my early ministry.

As a seventeen-year-old evangelist, I didn't have much of a repertoire. I had prepared a sermon on the rapture for the Sunday morning service of my first revival meeting, but at the last moment I felt the Lord redirect me to preach on the story from Luke 5 where Jesus told His future disciples, "Let down your nets." The disciples replied, "We fished all night and caught nothing. Nevertheless, at Your word, we will." So I preached on expecting something. Then on Sunday night I preached the sermon on the rapture.

On Monday I had a nervous breakdown, or at least it felt like one. I thought I preached the whole gospel in those two services; there was nothing left to preach. I'd preached it all. I prayed all day long, and the Lord gave me a scripture. I prayed every day for a new message. Monday night I preached on salvation, Tuesday on the baptism in the Holy Spirit, and Wednesday on divine healing. Then I had another meltdown because I thought that, in five services, I had preached everything there is to preach. On Thursday, God opened the Scriptures to me in a powerful way, and I realized that I could spend a lifetime preaching and never even touch the edge of the tremendous volume of truth there. From that day on, I have never worried about having enough to preach because there is just so much in the Scriptures.

When people ask about how I prepare sermons, I confess that I've never had a formal preparation procedure. I simply follow the old country preacher's advice: "Study yourself full, pray yourself hot, and preach yourself empty." I don't study to "get" sermons; I am always studying, always reading, always praying. It has never been a matter of saying, "Now, I'm going to make a sermon out of this." It's more like a flow of consciousness in terms of the awareness of what God is saying to me through the Scriptures.

That approach to preaching was combined with a powerful sense of enthusiasm. I seldom preached more than fifteen minutes. In the early days, I preached less than that because I felt that I should preach as hard as I could go until I ran out of breath. If you ran out of breath, you ran out of the anointing and it was time to quit. So there were times when I preached eight or ten minutes, but there was a wonderful anointing on those enthusiastic sermonettes. People got saved, healed, and baptized in the Holy Spirit.

I averaged praying three hours a day and fasting three days a week during those early years. I carried a library in the trunk of my car. Those boxes of books shaped my vision and outlook. I had books on prayer, missions, and evangelism, as well as classic books of Christian literature. Leonard Ravenhill, T. L. Osborn, and E. Stanley Jones were my constant companions. I read several hours a day. The time I spent in the Word, reading, and in prayer and fasting were the fuel of my passion. When I walked into a church and stood up to preach, an amazing anointing came upon me. Pastors and congregations recognized that something important was happening. I preached four hundred times one year.

My enthusiasm and lack of formal training sometimes produced hilarious results. I was preaching a revival at Riverview Assembly of God in Columbus, Georgia, my grandmother's church. She and several older women were sitting on the second, third, and fourth pews. This was a strong Pentecostal church of what we used to call "Mill Hill" people, not highly educated but wonderful, sincere, and fervent. I was praying and reading the Scriptures and got over to Habakkuk, the third chapter. I took the Scripture literally. Still following my regimen of reading the Scripture daily, praying, fasting, and seeking God, I read this passage that says, "God came from Teman, and the Holy One from mount Paran" (v. 3, KJV). I thought, "What is this? Everybody always says that God came from nowhere; God was always just there." Suddenly there it was—hidden in this obscure, prophetic book of only three chapters: "God came from Teman, and the Holy One from mount Paran."

A revelation exploded in my heart. The Scripture had described where God came from, so I stood that night and preached it. "God came from Teman," I said.

All the old people were giving each other puzzled looks and saying, "What? All the old preachers said that no one knew where God came from, but this seventeen-year-old lad has found where God came from—he has found the scripture." They rejoiced. Pastor Wetzel, a great, godly, and wise man, sat on the platform and smiled. He never said a word—just smiled. We had revival that night! They shouted and cried. Later, when I was at Southeastern, I discovered that this referred to the presence of God that moved from one place to the other. It was not talking about the origin of God.

A thirteen-year-old boy sat on the front row in that meeting. That boy's mother brought him to church every night, and we became friends that week. He later grew up and became a pastor. The boy's name was John Kilpatrick. When he got married a few years later, I was in his wedding. When he pastored the Brownsville Assembly of God in Pensacola, the church invested $500 a month into our ministry in India. Later John led one of the great church-based revivals of the 1990s that drew hundreds of thousands of people from around the world to Pensacola—a revival focused on the presence of God. As a preacher, you never know who may be sitting on the front row or what God will do with them.

I was receiving invitations to go lots of places. Fifteen months went by. It was the middle of August, and I was preaching a revival meeting in the southern Louisiana town of Thibodaux. I was eighteen years old. As I was praying that day, it seemed the Lord was telling me it was time to go to Southeastern Bible College, an institution dedicated to preparing young people with the call of God on their lives for ministry. I had six months of revivals scheduled. When this impression came over me, I balked: "I can't go to Southeastern. I've got six months of services scheduled. My heart is to go to India, not to Southeastern." I sensed the Lord telling me to call the pastors where I had scheduled the meetings and tell them I was interested in going to Southeastern. So I called each one of them, and everyone said, "Go to Southeastern."

Then I felt rejected. I thought, "They didn't want me to come in the first place." Middle children have such fragile egos! I felt like Abraham. God was calling me out! This was what I was supposed to do. So I finished that meeting in Thibodaux and went home to Pensacola, said goodbye to my family, and headed for Lakeland, Florida, where Southeastern was located. On the way, I drove to Cairo, Georgia, and preached there on a Wednesday night.

I arrived at Southeastern on a Monday. I had preached revival meetings in the Lakeland area, so I knew some of the faculty members and the registrar. I walked into the registrar's office and said, "I've come to go to Bible school."

He smiled and said, "Welcome, David, but you have to fill out an application."

I said, "But I'm not applying; I'm here."

"You still have to fill out an application."

I replied, "OK," and filled out the application.

Then he asked, "How much money do you want to put on your bill?" I asked him how much money he wanted. He said they asked for at least $50 with the application.

"OK, I have $50."

He said, "Did you stop in Cairo, Georgia, last Wednesday night and preach at the church?"

"Yes, I did." I told him that the $50 came from a little Methodist lady in the service named Mrs. Wiggim.

The registrar said, "Welcome, David. We knew you were coming. Mrs. Wiggim wrote and said, 'Little Brother David Grant is coming down there to go to Bible school, and I want to help him. Enclosed is a check for $1,000.'" This was just the beginning of a series of miracles, a confirmation that God was in this.

Southeastern was not a large school. It was certainly not the successful university it is today. The student body in 1964 numbered 350 students. They came from the farms and mill towns of the South. Most of their parents didn't have a lot in the way of earthly possessions. In the 1960s, the South was only beginning to emerge from a century of poverty. The parents and grandparents of these students had been saved in the revivals that swept the South during the Great Depression of the 1930s and in the healing revival of the 1940s and '50s. They were simple, hardworking people. The most important people in their world were not politicians or businessmen; they were the evangelists and pastors who proclaimed the Pentecostal message of Jesus as Savior, Healer, Baptizer in the Holy Spirit, and soon-coming King. For these folks, there could be no higher calling than the call to preach. So these simple people sent their best and brightest children to Bible college to learn how to be men and women of God.

Southeastern was more than a college; it was a spiritual boot camp. Every morning we went to chapel. Every evening at 7 p.m. we had "Quiet Time," a time for personal prayer and Bible study. Friday nights, we had a chapel service that often extended late into the evening. There were "Spiritual Emphasis Weeks" when the class schedule would be shortened to accommodate longer altar services where we could seek God and let Him speak to our hearts. The school was not primarily an academic institution; it was a place for spiritual formation. You came to meet God and become a man or woman of God.

I pitched myself headlong into campus life. I got involved in student government. Six weeks after enrolling, I was elected freshman class president. In my sophomore year, I was elected vice president of the student body. In my junior year, I was elected president. I even joined the choir; well, not exactly. I tried to join the choir. The director, a colorful and gifted character named Birdie Kovacs, quickly concluded that my vocal skills could be best utilized preaching when the choir went on tour.

But my real passion was for prayer. I started a freshman class prayer meeting. Most of the class met every Wednesday night and prayed from 7 to 9 p.m. The truth is, the school needed prayer. The previous spring, the school had gone through a crisis that brought the resignation of the president, caused more than one hundred students to leave school, and left the upperclassmen bitter and cynical. When we launched the Wednesday night prayer meeting, they made fun of us. "What do you think this is? Youth camp? You're here to learn theology and to get an education, not pray all the time." Their criticism didn't bother us a bit.

A few weeks later, we experienced a powerful campus revival. Classes were suspended for a week of prayer and fasting. Many of those young people had life-changing experiences in God's presence. Sixty-eight members of that class later went into the ministry—the highest percentage of any class in the history of the university. Many of the same upperclassmen who mocked us a few weeks earlier started slipping into the prayer meetings. That prayer revival changed our lives and the atmosphere of the school. It shaped our class. And it showed me that prayer really does change things, that it really can alter the landscape of a place. I believed that because I saw it happen.

I'm sure that my lifelong commitment to Bible schools was born in my own experience at Southeastern. I wanted young people in Southern Asia to have the same opportunity I had to experience God and become the persons God wanted them to be.

When I was a freshman, God spoke to me in an all-night prayer meeting. He said, "David, if you will give Me your life, I will break you in a million pieces, and I will feed you to a million children in India. As the little boy gave Me his lunch, and I took those five pieces of bread and broke them and fed thousands, I will take your life and I will break it into a million pieces."

It was one of those moments that changes you forever. I had discovered my purpose in life—to be broken bread.

I took every missions course I could. There I encountered one of the most influential people of my life, Ruth Breusch. Ruth was the daughter of two of the great pioneer Pentecostal missionaries to India, Christian and Violet Schoonmaker. The Schoonmakers had gone to India in the early 1900s. Her father had a vision for uniting the Pentecostal movement in India and began to pull missionaries and pastors together. He also had a powerful healing ministry. Sadly, Christian died before he was forty. Violet gave the rest of her life to India. Their daughter, Ruth, served as a missionary beside her. Toward midlife, Ruth married Percival Breusch, a very proper Englishman. God's calling brought them to Southeastern, where Percival tried vainly to instruct his charges in the mysteries of English grammar and composition. Ruth taught all the missions courses.

Ruth Breusch was deeply spiritual, and she had as strong and keen a mind as I have ever seen. She challenged her students to carefully examine the Scriptures, to think critically, and to express themselves clearly. When she lectured on the Book of Acts, it came alive. She was a hard taskmaster, and I don't believe I ever received an A in any class she taught. But "Sister" Breusch, as all of us called her, knew God, she knew missions, and she knew India. She became a cherished mentor and friend. I spent hours talking to her about missions theology. Ruth Breusch helped me to lay a biblical foundation for a life in ministry, of how we view the world and how we live in the world in the presence of God. I spent hours with her during my Southeastern years and later, reaping the benefits of her deep knowledge and insight.

One of the most profound lessons I learned from her was something she said to my wife, Beth, years after I graduated. She was talking to Beth about the key to reaching India with the gospel. "Without living and walking in the presence of an awesome God, we will never be effective sharing God with the Hindu and India. They will never respect our God. They live in a world of awareness of the spiritual in the One of Hinduism. We cannot offer them less."

Ruth Breusch was also a strong advocate for the indigenous church. She firmly believed that the New Testament pattern for establishing churches required that congregations become self-governing, self-sustaining, and self-propagating. For her, this meant that healthy churches could not be dominated by foreign leaders and their cultural norms. This was not a view shared by all missionaries. Many of them kept a tight rein on national pastors and evangelists by paying their salaries.

People throughout Africa and Asia who had lived under the domination of the European powers achieved independence in the years after the Second World War. India was the first nation to throw off foreign rule in 1947. When I went to college, new countries were being born every year. Not surprisingly, the fires of nationalism burned in the hearts of church leaders as well. These leaders appreciated what the missionaries had brought to them, but they knew that a church dominated by foreigners would always be alien to the culture and weak, that it could never fulfill the Great Commission. Having grown up under the colonial powers, they had known what it was to be "boys" their whole lives. Now that political freedom had come, they had no desire to live in colonial churches. Ruth Breusch came down squarely on the side of the indigenous church. I became a convert. Years later, when issues of control arose between American missionaries and national leaders, I could often feel Ruth Breusch looking over my shoulder and I knew what to do. Because of her, I always defended the Indian church leaders.

Ruth also taught me about mentoring. It is often said of teacher-student relationships, "Teacher for a day, teacher for life." Throughout the years of our friendship, she challenged me and corrected me like few other people in my life. When she thought I needed to think differently or change my approach, she would lean forward and say, "Now, David," and I would listen—and I'm still listening.

I held revivals almost every week throughout my four years at Southeastern. I averaged preaching seven times a week. I would jump in my car as soon as classes ended in the afternoon and drive to one of the many little churches in the small towns or out in the orange groves of Central Florida. I often returned to campus after midnight. Somehow I dragged myself out of bed every morning for classes and never missed a class or a chapel service in four years.

Very few of these churches were air-conditioned. It was hot—Central Florida hot. I'd be preaching away and occasionally swallow a mosquito or bug, but everybody was happy. In those days, you'd go to a church and they would invite you to preach on Sunday because someone in the church knew you or they had heard of you. After I finished preaching, either on Sunday morning or Sunday night, the pastor would take a vote of the congregation and say, "Do you want to run a revival meeting this week with Brother David? How many of you want to go all week?" People would raise their hands or not. It seemed like they always raised their hands. So we would start a revival meeting that night. I'd preach every night that week, and the next Sunday they would take another vote. "How many want to run another week with Brother David?" Sometimes we'd run every night for two or three weeks. People got saved, healed, filled with the Spirit, and stirred. It was a wonderful time.

Despite my schedule of nonstop revivals, I was still an active member of the Student Government Association. My sophomore year, Lowell Harrup, who later became one of my best friends, and his wife, Carol, were selected as the married students' representatives. Lowell and I clashed at every student government meeting. I was something of an activist and very much concerned about the professors and the theology being taught. Because I was an evangelist, I wanted a stronger emphasis on evangelism. I felt like the school was far too academic. It needed to be more spiritual. Lowell was brilliant, with a deep appreciation for the academic side, and regularly took the professors' side against me. I would take the anti-professor side against him.

My activism focused on the cafeteria, a perennial source of irritation at Southeastern during the 1960s. Students across America protested the Vietnam War and marched for civil rights. At Southeastern, we marched on the cafeteria. I was student body president and used the full powers of my office to get better food. We won a short-term victory.

That year I also worked in an orange juice processing plant. The plants shut down at midnight every Friday night for the weekend. They brought in crews to clean the machines between midnight Friday night and noon on Saturday. The cleaning crews worked twelve-hour shifts. Most of the crews came from Southeastern. I had other jobs too. I worked as a photographer for a while. I didn't really know anything about it, but I could get people to smile, and I made good money. I also had a paper route. I would throw papers on people's porches every morning at 5 a.m.

Southeastern was also a place to form lifelong friendships. When I went to Southeastern, it never occurred to me that God was bringing people into my life who would become friends and colleagues throughout my ministry. As I look back over the last fifty years, I am amazed at how God orders people's steps from many places to get them together.

David Daniels became my best friend at Southeastern and has been one of my closest friends through the years. We preached revivals, double-dated, and went to India together. We shared our dreams and our frustrations. David came from Wanchese, a fishing village on the Outer Banks of North Carolina. David's father owned a large fleet of shrimp boats on the Atlantic. He and his wife raised fifteen children, four of whom went into ministry. The "Wanchesers," as they were known at Southeastern, were a different breed. In the days before television and modern highways, they lived an isolated existence. They were tough and utterly resistant to the conventions and opinions of mainlanders.

Every August, a dozen or fifteen Wanchesers descended on Southeastern like a horde of invading barbarians. Tanned, barefooted, and wearing tattered shorts, they pushed the limits of Southeastern propriety. One of them ran afoul of the system and found himself in the president's office. The president could see there was not an ounce of repentance in the young man, so he dismissed him from the college. The young man reacted to the verdict by cartwheeling out of the office.

David Daniels (left) has been one of my closest friends since we attended Southeastern together. He also became a missionary and was mentored by Charles Greenaway, field director for Assemblies of God World Missions in Eurasia.

David Daniels was a Wancheser to his core. He was as tough and as much his own man as any of them. But he was more: he was the truest friend a man could have. An exceptional athlete, I'm sure David could have played basketball or football at any number of colleges. But he had a heart for God and a passion to preach the gospel.

I preached my first revival in Wanchese in 1970. It marked the beginning of a beautiful relationship. The Wanchese church has prayed for us and sown into our ministry for over fifty years. They have sent their best young people to work with us in India, including David's younger brother, Mark, and his wife, Cathy, who have worked with us for more than twenty years. After watching them for all these years, I'm sure that growing up in Wanchese taught them to be self-sufficient. I believe growing up on the stormiest stretch of coast in North America also taught them that storms are a part of life and that they will pass. Thank God for Wanchese.

Fellow missionary evangelists Wayne Francis (second from right) and David Daniels (right) and I (left) would show up anywhere in the world our mentor Charles Greenaway (second from left) asked us to go.

Chapter 5

THE CITY OF
DREADFUL NIGHT

WHEN I WAS seventeen, I made a vow to God not to marry until I was thirty. I don't recommend that. No one should make such a vow unless they sense specific direction from God. But I wanted to invest everything I had in missions for thirteen years.

I made another promise to God when I was seventeen, a faith promise. I told God I would give $300 a week to missions for thirteen years. By the end of those thirteen years, I had given $250,000 to missions out of my personal money. I didn't have a wife or kids, so I didn't have any bills. I didn't own a house or car. I gave everything I had to God, and God met every need. I had incredible friends. A car dealer provided me with a new car whenever I came home from India.

My brothers opened up their homes, and every one of them had a guest room that was David's room. My clothes hung in their closets. I did not own anything, but I had the call of God and the provision of God. I felt like a millionaire.

After I graduated from Southeastern, I drove straight to New Brockton, Alabama, where Charles and Mary Greenaway were visiting family. Charles was the Assemblies of God regional director for Eurasia, a region that covered eleven time zones from Vladivostok in the East to Greenland in the West. Most important to me, Charles Greenaway was responsible for Assemblies of God ministries in India. In those days, you didn't make appointments to see people in the South; you just dropped by. When I sat down in the house, I said, "Brother Greenaway, I'm ready to go to India." And it was Charles Greenaway who sent me to India to work with Mark Buntain. He opened the doors for me. He wrote to Mark Buntain and said, "I'm sending you a young evangelist named David Grant. He'll be a real blessing to you."

I didn't know Mark Buntain. Mark Buntain didn't know me. But Charles Greenaway sent me, so I headed out to India in 1969 at the age of twenty-three. In those days, air travel was much more expensive than it is today, meaning you didn't go to India for a week or two but rather for two or three months, even six months. The plan was for me to go to India and preach crusades throughout the country. An evangelistic crusade would last for eight days, Sunday to Sunday. I would preach every night.

When the time for my departure arrived, the whole Grant clan trekked out to the little airport in Pensacola. These were the days before TSA and extensive security, so the whole gang walked out to the gate. When they called the flight, Dad looked at us and said, "Let's pray."

I thought we would have a family huddle and Dad would mumble a short prayer, but that was not my father. At the top of his voice, he shouted, "David is going to India!" Five hundred people now knew I was going to India. He covered me with the blood of Jesus; he covered the plane, the pilot, the copilot, and the navigator. He covered everybody on the plane with the blood of Jesus. He worked the rapture and the second coming of Christ into the prayer. I don't remember being more embarrassed at any other time in my life.

We boarded the flight. The man next to me leaned over and said, "Was that your dad?"

When I nodded, he said, "I haven't heard a prayer like that in twenty-five years. My father prayed that same prayer over me when I was a boy. He died twenty-five years ago. I walked out of his funeral angry at God, and I have not darkened the door of a church since. But when your dad started praying, it all came back. I felt an arm around my shoulder as I have not felt it in twenty-five years. It was my father's voice I heard, and while your father prayed, I gave my heart to Jesus." By this time I was crying, and I heard the words of the song "The blood will never lose its power." I went to India with the conviction in my heart that the blood could touch anybody, anywhere.

When I landed in Calcutta (Kolkata), I was met at the airport by missionary Mark Buntain, who said brusquely, "Hurry up, boy. You're preaching in thirty minutes." Then he gave me a big bear hug. Mark, who was a big guy, lifted me off the floor. "Welcome, David, welcome to Calcutta. You're going to *love* it."

It is easier to loathe Calcutta than to love it. To borrow a phrase from Scottish poet James Thomson, Calcutta is truly "the City of Dreadful Night." Built on the delta of the Ganges River, Calcutta is about the worst location for a city on the planet. The city floods in rainy season, and it is no rare thing to wade through water up to your knees during the monsoons. Calcutta was built far enough away from the Indian Ocean that it's unusual to feel even the hint of a breeze. The air is often so thick and fetid that a Westerner can hardly breathe from April to October. Winston Churchill wrote to his mother after visiting Calcutta as a young cavalry officer, "I shall always be glad to have seen it—for the same reason Papa gave for being glad to have seen Lisbon—namely 'that it will be unnecessary ever to see it again.'"[1] British historian and politician Thomas Macaulay said, "Insects and undertakers are the only living creatures which seem to enjoy the climate."[2]

And yet Mark Buntain loved Calcutta with every fiber of his being. Mark had taken his wife, Huldah, and their baby girl, Bonnie, to India in the early years after India achieved independence from the British in 1947. The British may have built Calcutta, but they had not invested much in it for the last century. The "New Market" was built in the early days of the twentieth century. Despite the fact that more than twelve million people were jammed into Calcutta's sixty-four square miles—an area about the size of Washington, DC—it had been almost one hundred years since a new hospital was constructed. Nothing worked very well in Calcutta because the population was at least five times larger than the city could effectively support.

Mark had gone to Calcutta in 1954 to "fill in" for a missionary who had returned to the States on furlough. He was only supposed to be there until that missionary returned. But during that year, something happened to Mark Buntain: God broke his heart. He launched a one-man assault on Satan's kingdom in Calcutta. Over the next thirty-five years, Mark built the central Assemblies of God church in Calcutta to an attendance of more than four thousand every Sunday. He planted forty-three churches in East Bengal and built a Christian school in every location. School enrollment topped six thousand boys and girls. By the time Mark went to heaven, more than one hundred thousand students had attended the schools.

Mark's name became synonymous with feeding the hungry. The feeding programs started like so many of the outreaches Mark launched. One day a little girl fainted at her desk. When the teacher revived her, she asked the child how long it had been since she'd eaten. The little girl replied, "Three days." Mark decided right there to begin feeding every child in every school. When refugees from the war in Bangladesh flooded the city in 1969, many people threw up their hands in despair. Mark tried to feed them all.

Mark Buntain, shown here with me; my wife, Beth; and our daughter Rebecca, became like an older brother to me. He taught me that nothing is impossible if God is in it.

That was Mark. He heard the voice of God in the cries of the suffering. One night Mark received a call that a baby in the church had been rushed to the hospital with meningitis. The child had a raging fever when he arrived in the waiting area. The parents had been waiting for hours. It was clear to him that she would die unless someone attended to her quickly.

Mark took the child in his arms and went to the nurse in charge. "Somebody has to do something to help this child. She's going to die."

The nurse dismissed Mark and the child with a wave of her hand. "They're all going to die. What makes this child any different?"

Mark said later, "I knew that God told me right there that I had to start a hospital."

So Mark Buntain, who knew nothing about hospitals, started a hospital. It didn't matter that his denomination did not start hospitals—it, in fact, had a policy in place *not* to start hospitals. Mark had heard from God, and he would build a hospital. God would provide. And God did provide. Then he launched a nursing school. When he died, he was planning a medical school. No feasibility study or strategic planning process would ever have recommended building a hospital in Calcutta. To Mark, that was irrelevant—Mark had heard from God.

Mark was a mystic. He didn't really live in Calcutta; he lived in the presence of God. His body might be in India, but Mark's residence was in God. Mark Buntain prayed from the time he got out of bed in the morning until he went to bed at night. As a classical Pentecostal, when Mark prayed, it was usually in tongues.

Mark Buntain and I are standing outside the Royd Street Assemblies of God church in Calcutta, a city Mark loved and served for more than thirty-five years.

That is the man who embraced me at the airport. He became like an elder brother to me. Mark taught me that the heart of God is a heart for people. My legalistic Pentecostal upbringing had taught me that God demanded perfection and compliance. Mark showed me that the heart of the gospel is compassion. Mark also taught me that nothing is impossible if God is in it, and he taught me that you can fight for what you believe without being mean.

I learned something from Mark that they cannot teach you in a classroom or in a conference; I learned brokenness. My Southern upbringing instilled many wonderful qualities in me, like loyalty and honor and the meaning of family and place. But there's not much brokenness in the male-dominated culture of the South.

There is a lot of pride. It has been said that "being Southern means you never forget a kindness and never forgive an insult." Southern men don't believe they are as good as other men; they believe they're better than other men. My great-grandfather's generation fought on hundreds of battlefields to prove it. It didn't matter to Southerners that the Yankees beat them in that war; in their souls, they knew they were superior. And, for them, the war isn't over yet.

Brokenness is no part of Southern character, but it defined Mark Buntain. Mark lived broken before God. It kept God and the hunger for God number one in his life, and it protected him from presumption. A friend tells a story about Mark visiting in the home of a Midwest pastor. The pastor had found an album of Indian music, which he played during dinner. One particularly haunting piece was called "The Song of India." When Mark heard it, he began to weep. He asked the pastor to play it again. When it finished, Mark walked over to the stereo and put the song on auto-play. He then stretched out on the floor in the pastor's living room and began to pray for India. After an hour or so, the pastor rose from his chair and went to bed. When he returned to the living room the next morning, there was Mark, still on the floor weeping and praying. Young men and women often ask me the key to being successful in the ministry. Some of them are really looking for a magic bullet. I learned the key from Mark.

I also saw fragility in Mark. I was there when Mark

was hospitalized in Calcutta. Charles Blair, a great pastor from Denver, was with Huldah and me when Mark's doctor discussed Mark's condition. Blair looked at us and said, "Mark is burned out. He is exhausted. This is what we're going to do. Mark will get total rest for the next month. Huldah will run the ministry. David will preach at the church."

And that is what we did. I preached twelve services a week for the next three months. Huldah took care of the ministries and outreaches of the mission, and Mark got the rest he desperately needed.

Some Pentecostals can't admit the psychological and emotional struggles we all have. But like many of the great saints and mystics of Christian history, Mark sometimes fought to hold it together. To my knowledge, Mark's struggles have never been written about or even acknowledged. I can't imagine the pressures he lived under in Calcutta. I would be there for a few months and come home physically and spiritually exhausted; he spent thirty-five years there. The burden of a nation weighed on his soul, and the misery of millions of suffering people haunted him. We should not be surprised that at times the burden was more than Mark could bear. We should also not be surprised that the same Lord who cried out on the cross "My God, My God, why have You forsaken me" heard Mark's cry and healed him more than once.

When I arrived in Calcutta, Bangladesh was embroiled in civil war following their declaration of independence from Pakistan. Nine million refugees from there filled an already overcrowded Calcutta. They lived on the streets and in the city dump. They slept on the sidewalks. The city had no way to feed or care for them. The West stood by while hundreds died every night. I was awakened before dawn each morning by the sound of bells on the horses pulling the wagons that picked up the dead.

The city administration had laid sewer pipes alongside the streets awaiting installation, and the refugees moved into the sewer pipes. A sewer pipe, three feet in diameter, eight feet long, made a home for a refugee family.

I walked by one sewer pipe and saw that a man and his wife and two children lived there. The little girl might have been about five, the little boy about two. Early each morning the mother and dad would go off looking for food, work, anything, leaving those two little children standing in the opening of the sewer pipe. Every morning, they would wave at me as I walked by. The little girl wore a burlap sack. She had no shoes. Her hair was matted. The little boy wore nothing at all. They were just two little refugee kids from Bangladesh.

One morning the little girl mustered up her courage, stepped away from the end of the sewer pipe onto the sidewalk, and said to me in Bengali, "Mister, we're hungry. Please help us."

"I'll be back in a moment," I quickly responded. We were feeding fifty thousand children a day at that time. It was costing us ten cents a day to feed a child. One hundred dollars fed one thousand kids. I went down to the feeding program and said, "Give me the biggest plate you've got," and I headed back down the street a few moments later with a plate heaping with rice and vegetables. When I got back, the little girl and boy were standing at the end of that sewer pipe, and I handed the girl the plate of food. She smiled like it was Christmas and gestured to her brother to go into the sewer pipe. He stepped inside, then she crawled in after him.

As I stood and looked through the rags at the end of the sewer pipe, that five-year-old girl, with marks of hunger on her face, sat her baby brother down in front of her and began to feed him. For the next seven minutes, she fed him all he wanted. She never put a bite of food in her mouth. When he finished eating, he nodded, then she took what was left and ate it.

I stood there with tears running down my face, and I wanted to say to that little Bengali refugee girl, "I have never seen you in anything except a burlap sack. You don't own a pair of shoes. You don't have a ribbon for your hair. You are just a little refugee girl. You live in a sewer pipe, but you know more about giving than anybody I've ever met. You would not eat until you fed your brother first. And if God will help me, I'll never again sit down to eat until I feed somebody else first."

Calcutta is a hard place, a place that tears at your heart and eats at your guts. It assaults your senses and never leaves you. Many people find themselves paralyzed by the suffering. It is impossible to live and work in Calcutta and not be affected by it.

The civil war in Bangladesh left three million dead and five hundred thousand women raped.[3] In the fall of 1970 I worked in refugee camps with children who had been traumatized, unable to speak after seeing their mothers raped by Pakistani soldiers, their fathers murdered, and their brothers and sisters slaughtered. They stood there, staring in silent terror. I held babies who died in my arms. I remember one emaciated baby girl. I could see her heart beating inside her tiny chest. I held a milk bottle to her lips, but she didn't have the strength to suck. When her heart stopped, the nurse I was working with took her lifeless body out of my hands and said, "It was too late two days ago, David. They brought her in too late."

I became numb. I could no longer cry. I had no tears left. Something happened to my heart that day; my heart became hardened—hardened by man's inhumanity to man, hardened by the rape and the murder, and hardened by the needless suffering of so many children.

Then one day God broke through and said, "David, you are not responsible for all the pain and suffering in these refugee camps. Give that to Me. I went to the cross for the pain and sin and suffering. Let Me deal with it." Suddenly I was able to weep again because God took my heart of stone and gave me a heart of flesh.

That word from the Lord sustained me for a long

time, maybe four or five years, but Calcutta wears you down like swimming against a riptide that never ends or an undertow that constantly pulls your legs out from under you. No matter how much you pray, no matter how faithful you try to be, after a while it exhausts you.

I reached the breaking point one morning in 1975. Someone laid a refugee baby on our doorstep in the middle of the night. They must have known we were believers and would take care of the child. The dogs got to the baby before we did and tore the baby to pieces. Something snapped inside of me that morning when I looked at the mutilated body of that Bengali refugee baby.

I was on my way to a 6 a.m. prayer meeting, but I didn't go to prayer meeting that morning. I went back up to my room and vomited. I threw myself on the floor and said, "God, why did You let that baby die?" That was a mistake because God did not let the baby die. But I was distraught, haunted by the gruesome sight. A few minutes later, I asked God to forgive me, and I preached that night. For months I was like a zombie—no tears, no feeling, nothing. My enthusiasm for life and ministry was gone. I just went through the motions. I prayed for people. God even healed people, but I was dead inside.

However, Calcutta was not all suffering, dirt, and despair. I discovered dimensions of grace during my years there that I had not seen in America. A few days after I arrived in Calcutta, Mark took me to meet a friend of his, a little Catholic nun who was all of four feet ten inches tall. Her face wrinkled into the biggest smile you have ever seen when Mark introduced us.

"Mother, this is my friend, David Grant."

She enfolded my hands in both of hers and said the same thing Mark had said at the airport: "Welcome to Calcutta. You're going to love it."

When I looked into the face of Mother Teresa and saw a face that was warm, welcoming, and affirming, I realized God was present even in this "City of Dreadful Night." That realization would be tested again and again through the years, but my encounter with the joyful nun stayed with me.

Agnes Gonxha Bojaxhiu, the woman who became Mother Teresa, went to India in 1929. After teaching for twenty years, the suffering and misery of Calcutta's poor increasingly distressed her. Sister Teresa experienced what she later described as a "call within a call" while traveling by train on her annual retreat. "I was to leave the convent and help the poor while living among them. It was an order. To fail would have been to break the faith."[4]

Beth and our daughters, Rebecca and Jennifer, met Mother Teresa in Calcutta at the Mother House, where she once lived. Mother Teresa was a woman who walked and lived in prayer as she ministered to the poor.

It has been said that *Sister* Teresa became *Mother* Teresa in that moment. She began working in 1948 with what she called "the poorest of the poor," tending to the needs of the destitute and starving. Many people have ministered to the poor, but few have ever identified with the poor as she did. Mother Teresa exchanged the traditional habit of her order for a simple white cotton sari decorated with a blue border. She adopted Indian citizenship and then ventured out into the slums.

Mother Teresa opened the first Home for the Dying in 1952 in space made available by the city. Those brought to the home received medical attention and were afforded the opportunity to die with dignity.[5] Her critics, including some missionaries, could not see the point in a city where hundreds of the poor died every day. "A beautiful death," she replied, "is for people who lived like animals to die like angels—loved and wanted."[6]

Perhaps more than anyone I have ever known, Mother taught me that every person's life is of infinite value to God, that God has no throwaway children. Calcutta causes some people to sink into despair; others discover the grace and mercy of God. I know; I have experienced both the despair and the grace.

As I look back on fifty years in India, what I remember most is not the dirt, the masses, or the heat. What I remember most are the people. When I close my eyes to pray or drift off in memory, I see faces. I see Mark, Mother Teresa, and the little girl at the sewer pipe who showed me the face of God in Calcutta. I also see the face of the baby who died in my arms and the mutilated face of the baby on our doorstep. I think I have learned more from those faces than from all the theology books I read in seminary.

I remember one Christmas when I discovered the meaning of the incarnation in the face of a child. Beth and I were walking to church on Christmas Eve to preach for a young pastor who was planting a new congregation. He, his wife, and their three-year-old son lived in one room. On the way to the service, I walked by a shop and saw a tricycle in the window. It was the first tricycle I had seen in India. I had an overwhelming urge to buy that tricycle. Beth has always been the practical partner in our marriage. She said, "I think they can use the money more than they can use a tricycle, David. Let's give them the money."

I said, "No, I have to buy that tricycle."

I walked into the shop and asked the price. The proprietor told me $15, and I said, "I'll take it."

I picked up the tricycle, and we headed for the pastor's house. When we walked into that one-room apartment, I set the tricycle on the floor. The pastor's little son screamed, "Momma, my tricycle has come."

He ran over and jumped on it and began to spin around the room. His mother asked my wife, "Why did you bring him a tricycle for Christmas?"

And Beth, who spends a lot of time apologizing for me, said, "I thought perhaps we should have given you money instead, but David wanted to buy the tricycle."

"No, that's good," she said. "For three months he has prayed for a tricycle for Christmas. Yesterday he had a fever, and I went to his bed and he said, 'Momma, Jesus was just in my bed, and Jesus told me I was going to have a tricycle for Christmas.' I thought it was the fever and he was hallucinating, but I touched him, and his fever was gone, and I walked away from his bed crying. I asked myself, 'Now what are we going to do? He thinks he's seen Jesus, and Jesus has promised him a tricycle, and tomorrow is Christmas Eve and we do not have any money.' Then you walk through the door and set a tricycle on the floor. That tricycle did not come from you, it came from Jesus, in answer to a little three-year-old boy's prayers."

When the pastor's wife said that, God spoke to my heart and said, "David, ever since you found that baby that was killed, you have blamed Me. In your heart of hearts, you have blamed Me and you have said that I don't hear the cries of the children. I wanted to show you that I hear every cry. I'm looking for somebody who will be My hand to deliver the tricycle in answer to prayers."

I began to weep on that Christmas Eve. And if you think I'm embarrassed at weeping, you are wrong because I can remember when I could not cry. I can remember when my heart was like a stone, and I can remember when I preached and I prayed and I felt nothing.

I see other faces. I see the face of a young man we put through Bible college. Forty years ago, a dollar a day would pay to put a young man or young woman through Bible school. It was a great investment—just a dollar a day to train a young preacher. When David Mohan graduated from Southern Asia Bible College, we helped him rent a room for $30 a month. He started a new church with seven people. Today New Life Assembly of God in Madras (Chennai) numbers more than sixty thousand members and has launched hundreds of satellite churches.

David is just one face; I can think of hundreds more. I spent most of my time preaching crusades in those early days. We had some great crusades. Crowds of ten thousand were common. I preached the length and breadth of India. I was down South in Tamil Nadu on my first or second trip to India, in a village miles into the jungle, staying in a hut next to the pastor's house, when I became ill with fever. As I lay on a bamboo mat, I felt paralysis come into my legs. I had the distinct impression that I could die. I was miles from a doctor and a day or more from a hospital. Unless God touched me, there was nothing anyone could do.

In those days before cell phones—in fact, before most pastors even had telephones in their homes—the best way to communicate with the outside world was to send a telegram. I asked the pastor to send a telegram to my dad back in Pensacola and tell him about my situation.

Before the telegram got to Dad, a lady in the church called him in the middle of the night and told him she had a vision of David lying in a bamboo hut in India, that he had a high fever and was in danger of dying, and that she needed to pray. Dad called everybody in the church and asked them to pray for me. The Pentecostals of that day talked a lot about "praying through," which means when the Holy Spirit prompts you to pray, you stay with it until you sense a release or a breakthrough. That phrase, "praying through," captures an attitude and way of life. After a time of prayer Dad was sure he had prayed through and that I was going to be fine, that Jesus had healed me.

Dad sent me a telegram before he read the one I sent

to him. It said, "We know you are sick. We've prayed and you're going to be okay." I asked the pastor to lay the telegram on my chest. I laid my hand on that telegram and claimed my healing. It was the middle of the afternoon when Dad's telegram arrived. I felt the fever leave my body, and strength came back when the pastor laid that telegram on my chest. I got up, went to the crusade, and preached on the baptism of the Holy Spirit. The village had never had an outpouring of the Holy Spirit. That night scores of people received the fullness of the Holy Spirit.

Despite moments like the one in that little village, I was not in India very long before I realized the task of reaching the nation with the gospel was more than any one person could possibly accomplish. Hundreds would respond every night to the invitation to follow Jesus. But people were being born faster than we could reach them. At the rate we were going, we would never reach all of India for Christ.

The Assemblies of God was a Bible school movement. Wherever Assemblies of God missionaries have gone in the world, they planted churches and started Bible schools because they realized that even though foreigners played an important role in establishing churches in a nation, it would take the people from that country to reach their people. That challenge was magnified in India with its exploding population.

When I went to India, there were already several fine Bible schools in the country. Alfred Cawston launched

Southern Asia Bible College in 1954. Mark Buntain founded a Bible school in Calcutta to train Bengali pastors. But if one person could not meet the challenge of India, neither could one or two schools; it would take dozens of Bible schools training students in the major languages of the subcontinent. So, over the last fifty years, we have helped establish more than one hundred Bible colleges in India. The graduates of those Bible schools have been in the vanguard of church growth in India. They have planted thousands of new congregations and brought two million believers into the kingdom.

Here I am with graduating students at Bethel Bible College in Punalur, India, the oldest Assemblies of God Bible college outside the United States. I preached the graduation there for twenty-five consecutive years.

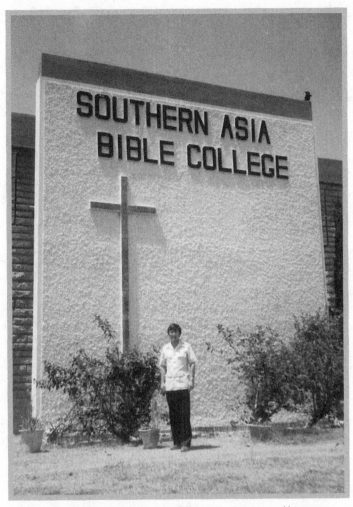

I developed a lifelong commitment to Bible school education and have seen Bible colleges such as Southern Asia Bible College raise up amazing leaders throughout Southern Asia, including many who are dear friends.

Chapter 6

ON THE SHOULDERS OF GIANTS

NONE OF US succeeds alone or ministers alone. We stand on the shoulders of those who have gone before, as the apostle Paul wrote to the Corinthians when they got caught up in cults of personality. My life has been immeasurably enriched by missionary mentors who went before me and poured their lives into mine. They shared their hearts and imparted their vision. They modeled mountain-moving faith. I watched them navigate bone-crushing disappointments. They were men of God and men for God. I cannot imagine my life without Charles Greenaway, Phil Hogan, Andrew McCabe, and David Stewart Sr. No story of my life could be complete without mentioning theirs.

Charles Greenaway

Charles Greenaway was one of a kind. Bold, brash, and with the courage of a lion, if Greenaway thought it, he said it. Greenaway was never far from the streets that spawned him.

That wild streak in Greenaway, which offended the gentle sensibilities of some, attracted entrepreneurs to the region he oversaw. They were magnetically drawn to him. He gave them freedom and backed them up when they rubbed other missionaries the wrong way.

When the Greenaways flew to West Africa, it was 1944, and even though the Italians had surrendered and the Germans were in retreat across Europe, there was still a war and German submarines prowled the Atlantic. H. B. Garlock was the Assemblies of God field director for Africa, and he told Greenaway before he left that if he received a telegram upon arriving in Africa, it would be with orders to return to the States. That was a strategic mistake. When the Greenaways landed in Africa, there was a telegram waiting for Charles. He shoved it in his pocket and didn't read it. In fact, he never read it! When Garlock came to visit Greenaway after the war, he asked if he had received the telegram. Greenaway responded that he had but that he'd never read it.

And yet Greenaway was more than a maverick; he was one of the greatest pioneer missionaries the Assemblies of God ever produced. When Charles and Mary went out to Togo, there weren't many Christians in the areas outside the cities. Most Western missionaries around the world lived in "compounds," small settlements of missionaries walled off from the surrounding populations. Many of them never assimilated the cultures of their new homes. Their ministries were blunted by the distance they kept from the people they were called to serve.

Frequently, they waited for people to come to them. Greenaway would have none of that. He would often point out that the first two letters in the word *gospel* were G-O, go! And Charles Greenaway went. He traveled to hundreds of villages, preaching outdoors, instructing new Jesus followers, and organizing churches.

For two generations, Greenaway was Assemblies of God missions in the Southeastern US. He preached in churches, youth rallies, camps, district councils, and missions conventions throughout the region. Hundreds of missionaries could testify that God called them to the mission field in a service where Charles Greenaway preached. One of the most memorable moments of my young life took place when Charles Greenaway preached in my dad's church in Pensacola, Florida. That was the night I stepped into the offering plate and never stepped out.

I have often marveled at how the Southeast took to Greenaway. He was the antithesis of everything Southern. In a region where courtesy and politeness were cardinal social virtues, Charles had a gift for the outrageous and the shocking. I'm sure his wife, Mary, was a large part of it. She was an elegant, refined Southern lady. She made Charles easier to digest. Mary's father, Dan Dubose, was one of the great revival preachers of the early Pentecostal outpouring. He had established scores of churches in Alabama and Florida. But there was something deeper. Southerners loved big personalities and they loved powerful preachers. Charles Greenaway was both. Greenaway didn't really have missionary services; he had one-night revivals with a missions offering.

Here I am standing with two men who greatly impacted my life and ministry (from left): Mark Buntain, founder of the Assemblies of God (AG) Mission in Calcutta, and Charles Greenaway, missionary pioneer and leader of AG World Missions in Eurasia.

Greenaway's strength came from his mother and his Irish upbringing. His father died when Charles was very young, leaving his mother with six mouths to feed. She had no education and no marketable skills. She had no way to take care of all her children. In the days before the social welfare programs that now provide food and medical care for dependent children, many mothers were forced to send their children to live with relatives, put them up for adoption, or let the county take them. Charles' mother didn't have anyone to help, so she decided to give Charles to the county. He was the oldest, and Charles' mother probably thought he could handle it. She wanted to say a last prayer over Charles and kiss him before he went away. She gathered them in a circle and said a prayer. As she did, a conviction came into her spirit that she must not send Charles away but instead believe God to provide for them as a family. At just that moment, the woman from the county agency walked up to her door, and Sister Greenaway told her what she had decided.

The woman could not believe what she was hearing. "How can you do such a thing? You don't have a job. You don't have any skills. You have no one." Charles' mother looked at her, raised her fist toward heaven, and said, "We're gonna make it. We might not look like much when we get there, but we're gonna make it." And they did. God took care of them. The Greenaways never missed a meal through the Great Depression. Years later I met Charles Greenaway's mother and could see her strength and faith. But I would catch glimpses of her from time to time when Greenaway was in a tough spot and he would set his jaw, raise his fist, and say, "We're gonna make it. We might not look like much when we get there, but we're gonna make it."

Many missions agencies today have little room for a character like Charles Greenaway. But it took people like "Brother Greenaway," who had a calling burned into their heart, who were strong enough and stubborn enough to stay with it to establish the gospel where it had never gone before. I've never been as stubborn or as pugnacious as Charles, but he gave me a confidence that, if God is with us, "We're gonna make it. We might not look like much when we get there, but we're gonna make it."

All that said, Charles had a tender side that expressed itself with children. I can still see him sitting on the floor with Rebecca, Jennifer, and other missionary kids telling them riddles. He would ask for a guitar and sing "Here, Rattler, Here," and they adored him. When Greenaway was with kids, he didn't pay much attention to the adults in the room. He focused on the little ones.

Charles and Mary died within a couple of days of each other in a hospital in Dothan, Alabama, in 1993. Hundreds of people, some in their eighties and nineties, jammed the church for Charles' homegoing. I had the privilege to be one of the twelve speakers at the funeral and to receive the offering. The funeral procession to the cemetery stretched out for more than a mile. Alabama state troopers stood at attention and saluted as the hearse went through each intersection. It was a tribute fit for a general. Greenaway would have loved it.

PHIL HOGAN

J. Philip Hogan was a classic World War II generation leader. He grew up on a ranch in Colorado where he learned to ride and rope. Nothing relaxed Hogan as much as saddling up his horse at the end of a tough week in the office and spending a few hours in the saddle. One Saturday, he invited me to join him—actually, it was more like an order. After a bone-jarring ride around his ranch, Hogan pulled up on the reins. The horse stopped, and Hogan leaned out over the pommel of his saddle, wiped his brow, and said, "You know, David, I didn't take this job to make friends."

I looked at him and said, "Well, Brother Hogan, you've been successful."

This goes to the heart of who Hogan was. Like the soldiers who stormed the beaches at Normandy, or slogged their way up the Italian peninsula, or fought in the jungles of the Southwest Pacific during World War II, Phil Hogan was focused on the job at hand. He didn't care what anyone thought about him. He would do his assigned task and leave the results for the Lord to judge.

Hogan believed that missions had to be run by missionaries, by people who had been through the trials and tribulations of missionary life. They were the only people who could be trusted to make the best decisions.

Phil Hogan was more than a naysayer; he was a great missionary strategist, even though he only spent three years on the field. Hogan went out to China after World War II, but his career as a missionary to China was cut short when the Communists threw the missionaries out of the country in 1950 following their victory over the Nationalists. Hogan had a strategic grasp, a view of the field that Napoleon called "the eye of genius." He oversaw explosive growth around the world, especially in Latin America and Africa.

The growth of the Hogan era came as the result of a dramatic shift in strategy and the deployment of missionary personnel. When Phil Hogan took the reins, most missionaries were posted in rural areas in leprosariums, schools, and orphanages. Hogan looked at the explosive growth of population and cities in the developing world and realized we were not deployed to maximum effect. Two major initiatives defined the Hogan years in Assemblies of God missions: planting churches and starting Bible schools. Hogan believed that every major city in the world needed a great evangelistic center to reach the lost, disciple new believers, and send out laborers into the harvest. He focused on starting Bible schools to train pastors, evangelists, and missionaries.

The scope of his achievement is mind-boggling. When Hogan took over, and be assured that Hogan *took over*, the Assemblies of God had fewer than one million members outside the United States. By the time he retired, that number had jumped to more than fourteen million. Today it exceeds sixty-five million. The number of missionaries grew from 750 to almost 1,500. The growth of churches was spectacular, from 13,000 to more than 110,000. It is hard to imagine that happening without Phil Hogan's singular focus and determination.

Some of Hogan's critics have downplayed his role, arguing that he led Assemblies of God missions in the midst of a great global outpouring. The fact of global revival is true; but no other evangelical missions agency saw anything comparable to the growth of the Assemblies of God in that period. It's impossible to separate that growth from the man God used to lead it.

A keystone of Phil Hogan's vision has not received much attention in the United States but was critical to the future of the Assemblies of God globally.

Throughout most of the twentieth century, Springfield had led Assemblies of God fellowships globally. As General Councils were established in nation after nation, Hogan could see the day coming when the national churches would want to relate to the United States on a more equal footing, as brothers not as children. With this in mind, he established the World Assemblies of God Fellowship. He recruited the pastor of the largest Assemblies of God church in the world, David Yonggi Cho of the Yoido Full Gospel Church in Seoul, South Korea, to help him build it. Together the two of them threw their energies into the project. What Hogan envisioned has come to pass: the national churches are full partners with the American church, and the chairman of the group is usually from somewhere other than the United States. The leading churches are now in the developing world, not in North America. That may be Hogan's most lasting achievement.

Phil Hogan was my friend, my mentor, and my defender. I could not have done what I've done without the freedom and support he gave me. He protected me. That doesn't mean he didn't "reprove, rebuke, and exhort." Hogan took me to task more than once.

ANDREW McCABE

Few people outside the missionary family ever hear of Andrew McCabe, who gave nearly fifty years to orphan boys in Nawabganj, India. Andrew was a soft-spoken, unassuming Scot born "under canvas," as he described it, to missionary parents in North India in the 1920s. Andrew's family lived in a tent for his first two years of life, his father often walking through the hills of North India as he went from village to village sharing the good news about Jesus.

Andrew fought in the British Army during World War II, returning after the war to pick up where his parents had left off. He took over an orphanage in the Himalayan foothills at Nawabganj in 1950. Under his leadership, it grew to more than fourteen hundred boys. Most of the boys were Nepalis whose families could not care for them. When it was illegal for a Nepali citizen to publicly declare himself or herself to be a Jesus follower, many of Andrew's "boys" rose to positions of influence in the Nepali government, army, and police force.

My mentor Andrew McCabe (right) was a missionary in north India and was honored by the Queen of England for his service to the children of India and Nepal. George Varghese (left), director of Global University for India, was a great friend and partner.

Many of the boys were brought to Andrew as babies, but Andrew did not wait for the boys to be brought to him; often he would go and find them. I don't remember how many times I called Andrew's home and asked for him, only to hear his wife, Evelyn, say, "Oh, David, Andrew isn't here. He's out taking a walk." This meant he was walking through his beloved Himalayan foothills, partly because it energized him but partly because he would likely come home with another boy from the streets or one whose parents could not care for the child. When Andrew went for a walk, he might be gone for two or three weeks.

Andrew wasn't much of a fundraiser. In fact, he hated raising money. He hated talking about money. He was very much in the faith tradition of missions. Andrew believed to his bones that God was his source and that all he needed to do was share the needs with his Father. The boys at the Nawabganj orphanage never missed a meal. Andrew McCabe believed God, and God showed Andrew that He was good for it.

During a ministry trip (from left) Andrew McCabe, David Daniels, and I took a break from driving on a north India road to grab something to eat out of the trunk of our car.

I first met Andrew in 1970 and was captured by his humility, stability, and common sense. Over my years in India, I found Andrew to be a faithful friend and reliable counselor. I remember when we started our quarterly magazine, *Today's India*, and Andrew read a profile of one of the Indian leaders. Andrew came to me and said, "Brother David, we must be very careful about the stories we tell." I wondered what he was driving at. Maybe he was worried about the story ending up on the wrong desk in India. He went on, "I'm concerned that the enemy will use this as an occasion to cause our brother to become proud and that will open him to greater problems." I didn't know what to say. In his gentle, kind way, Andrew spoke the heart of God.

When I think of Andrew, I can hear him saying grace at one of our area retreats in the late '90s. Just before he said amen, Brother Andrew added, "And remember the poor." It was how he closed every prayer he ever prayed. Andrew McCabe never forgot them, nor did the Father to whom Brother Andrew prayed.

Andrew was never honored at a General Council, never wrote a book, never appeared on television. But he wrote thousands of "living epistles" in the lives of the young men he served. It is interesting to note that Andrew's lifetime of contribution came to the attention of the Queen of England, who awarded Andrew with the Most Excellent Order of the British Empire (GBE) in 1991. This simple man, so averse to publicity, was given the highest recognition in the British Commonwealth.

DAVID STEWART SR.

It's hard to believe that Dave Stewart and I have worked together for fifty years. Dave is the senior man among Assemblies of God missionary personnel in Southern Asia. A tall, courtly Virginian, he has the manners and grace of a bygone era. However, if that is the only image of Dave you have, you would be missing the essence of the man. Dave Stewart is a true father with a heart for people and a keen eye for young men and women with potential, as he showed when he recruited David Mohan to join him in planting the church in Madras in 1971.

Dave feels personally responsible for everyone he comes into contact with. Near the start of Dave's missionary career, his travels took him out into the countryside on a particular road. There was a great old tree on that road whose branches spread like a canopy. Under those branches sat an old beggar. Dave passed him every time he drove on that road. He never talked with the man but would often smile or wave as he passed him. After some months, Dave noticed that the old beggar was gone. He inquired of some people standing nearby. "He has died," came the terse response. Dave realized he had never talked to the beggar about Jesus. The weight and finality of the man's passing into eternity without Christ pressed hard on Dave's spirit. He resolved to never let another opportunity pass without sharing the one message that can change a life.

In a country with more than a billion people, where

the masses crowd each other on the streets of every city, it's easy to lose sight of the individual. David Stewart never did. Neither did Andrew McCabe. Their hearts for the one lost sheep speak to me now. When I'm tempted to deal with a problem from an administrative viewpoint, I can see Andrew surrounded by his boys at Nawabganj or Stewart towering over a crowd, reminding me that God cares for the one lost sheep and that He searches for it until He finds it.

David Stewart Sr., shown here ministering to pastors during a conference, was a missionary statesman and my brother in spirit.

Chapter 7

TRIVANDRUM

LIKE MOST PEOPLE, there are moments when I'm keenly aware of God's hand on my life, but one of the most dramatic of those moments came in the South Indian city of Trivandrum in the early 1970s. I was in South India preaching three times a day in Kerala State in outdoor meetings with Ernie Sorbo. We went back to Ernie's house every night. It was hot, in a way only India can be hot—over 100 degrees every day. Ernie and I were in the jungle, and I contracted dysentery, which is the missionary's disease. If you get two missionaries together in almost any part of the world, they will start telling each other dysentery stories in about the first five minutes. In just a matter of days, I had gotten down to 105 pounds. I'd been preaching for ninety days without a single day off. The next day, I was to have my first day off and then fly out the following day to Madras. I went to bed about four in the morning, sick with dysentery and exhausted.

Ernie Sorbo (right) was a pioneer missionary and church planter in South India who mentored me in working closely with national pastors and leaders.

In those days, all the flights were on Indian Airlines—old Boeing 737s on the big routes and little British World War II–era, forty-passenger turbo props on the short routes. None of the turbo prop planes had computer systems. You made your reservation weeks in advance, and there were always lots of people on standby. It was nearly impossible to change a ticket.

I awakened after being in bed for just a few minutes with this feeling that I had to get up, get on the plane, and go to Madras. I tried to go back to sleep, but the feeling wouldn't stop. I said, "Lord, if this is You, and I don't know if it is, but if this is You, I'm sick and I can't go. I've preached every single day for ninety days. I'm sick with dysentery, and I'm down to 105 pounds." But the feeling just wouldn't go away. My bed turned to concrete. So at 4:30 a.m. I got up, went to Ernie's room, and said, "Brother Sorbo, I've got to go to Madras today." He replied, "You can't go to Madras." I said, "I know I can't, but I'm going out to the airport anyway. I'll get a taxi."

"Oh, no, no," he said. "I'll take you." Ernie got up and drove me out to the airport. I tried to check in, but the agent said, "There are no seats. Your reservation's for tomorrow. Please come tomorrow."

I said, "No, I'm going to sit here, and if a seat comes open, please let me know." I sat down, and half an hour later they were getting ready to board the flight when the agent came over and said, "I don't know what happened, but there's a seat open if you want to go." I said, "No, I don't want to go, but I'm going to go."

I got on the plane, flew to Madras, and checked into the hotel, where I promptly went to bed. The next morning, the manager, who knew me well, knocked on my door and asked, "Mr. Grant, why did you come yesterday?" I said, "I don't know why. I just came." He said, "This morning's flight crashed into a mountain and killed everybody on board, and they just released the names of the passengers." For some odd reason, my name was still on the passenger list. "Your name was on the list, but you came yesterday. Why?" I said,

"I don't know why. I just felt that God stirred my heart to come yesterday."

I was flabbergasted. My intended plane had crashed, and everyone on board was dead. Then I realized God had awakened me. I was not supposed to be on that plane. God had more work for me to do.

There's a mystery to this story that I have never fathomed. Why did God do that? I was spared, and all those people died. But that's the story. Many of the Indian leaders saw it as an indication that God's hand was on my life. When they introduced me, they would say, "This is the man who missed the flight that crashed and killed everybody on board." On the other hand, even though I told the story for almost a year, I developed a phobia about dying in a plane crash because I told it so much. So I stopped telling it.

That moment has stayed with me for more than forty-five years. Whatever questions I had then, I know that God didn't want me on that plane. He stirred me at 4:30 in the morning to keep me off that plane. I suppose that's one reason I've never worried much about my personal safety. Since that night, I knew, like Peter in Herod's jail, that I have an angel assigned to my care. When I miss a plane or a train, when I'm detained for a meeting, I don't worry. I know God is watching over me, and I'm not going to heaven until He takes me home.

My friend Mark Bliss, one of the greatest and godliest men I've ever known, lost three children in a car accident in Tehran. Beth lost her first husband in an accident when he was in his twenties. I know wonderful people who look at situations like this and ask, "Why?" I have asked this question myself. Many times, I don't have good answers for those struggling to get through such moments. But I know God watches over us and protects us. I live under that umbrella of protection every day of my life, even when things don't go the way I want them to go, and perhaps especially when they don't go the way I planned them. That's the enduring lesson of Trivandrum.

In my early days in India, I traveled the length and breadth of the nation, preaching crusades that often drew tens of thousands of people.

Here I am at a joyful church dedication with church leaders and colleagues.

Chapter 8

MARRYING A WIDOW

MADE A VOW when I was seventeen not to marry until I was thirty. I don't recommend that. Don't make any vow unless God specifically speaks to you. I won't say that it was always easy; it wasn't. As I moved into my late twenties, I found myself thinking more and more about getting married. I dated some wonderful young women. But I couldn't see any of them in the family picture. I knew it would take a woman of intelligence, wisdom, spiritual depth, and strength to survive India.

While preaching a youth camp in Pennsylvania when I was twenty-nine, I walked onto the platform and saw a young woman playing the piano. I asked the leader sitting beside me, "Who's that young woman? She's my type." He smiled and said, "Beth Shaffer. Her husband's leading the worship." That was the story of my life. At twenty-nine, the young women who caught my eye were already married. That night I met Brian and Beth Shaffer.

Brian was minister of music and minister of youth at a large church in Wilmington, Delaware. Beth served as the principal of the Christian school. They were both twenty-five. Beth was from Savage, Maryland, a small town located almost exactly halfway between Baltimore and Washington, DC. The three of us became great friends.

As anyone who knows me can testify, I love to tease. Sometimes it's not in the best taste. One day I looked at Brian and said, "Brian, if anything ever happens to you, I'm going to marry Beth." Brian laughed. We would probably be laughing about it today except that Brian died in an accident six weeks later, and that girl—who would later become my wife—became a widow.

I don't always understand the things of God, but I have learned to trust Him, even when I don't understand Him. Several weeks after the youth camp ended, Beth was playing the piano in their apartment during her devotions one day when an incredible sense of sadness came over her. She was playing one of her favorite songs, "I Have Decided to Follow Jesus." Suddenly the Spirit of God spoke to Beth and said sing the next verse: "Though none go with me, still I will follow; though none go with me, still I will follow; though none go with me, still I will follow; no turning back, no turning back." Beth felt the Spirit ask her, "If you have to go alone, will you follow?"

Through her tears, Beth said, "Jesus, I don't want to go alone, but I will. I will follow You even if I have to go alone." Six weeks later, a policeman knocked on her door and said, "Mrs. Shaffer, your husband has died in an accident." Beth says that while she felt overwhelming sadness, a peace came over her and a sense that God had prepared her.

The church asked her to stay and assume Brian's responsibilities. Beth was now principal of a Christian school, minister of music, and youth pastor to one hundred teenagers. When Beth left the church two years later, they hired three men to take her place.

I returned from India months later and heard of Brian's death. I called Beth almost immediately to see how she was doing. I will never forget her response. She said, "David, Brian belonged to God, not to me. I belong to God; it's all His. Our lives are like currency in the hands of God. He can spend us as He pleases. We don't tell Him how to spend our lives; He spends us in life and even in death."

Beth's sense of abandonment to God was both powerful and disconcerting. All my life I had heard people talk about "*my* wife, *my* husband, *my* children, *my* house, *my* car, *my* money, *my* ministry, *my* vision, *my* dream." Everything centered on them. Suddenly I was listening to a young woman saying, "It's all His."

I began to call Beth once a month, at first as a friend.

Then I called her once a week, then every day. Two hundred phone calls and one year later, I was praying and said, "God, I'm thirty-one years old, and for thirteen years I've given every dime I've made to missions. I'm willing to be single all my life if that's Your will, but if You ever want me to get married, I have a recommendation for You. There's a young widow in Philadelphia named Beth Shaffer."

The moment I called her name in prayer, God said, "That's the girl you're going to marry."

I grabbed the phone and called my dad in Pensacola, Florida. "Dad, I'm getting married." He said, "To whom? I didn't know you were going with anybody."

I said, "Well, I'm not exactly going with her."

"What is she like?" he asked.

"She's wonderful."

"What does she look like?"

I said, "She's beautiful! But I haven't seen her in two years. And the last time I saw her, she was married to someone else."

He said, "I'll be praying for you." I'm sure Dad thought his son had spent too much time in the Indian sun.

I was leaving for India the next afternoon, but I thought if I could get to Philadelphia for lunch, we could settle the issue. I called Beth that night and asked her if she was free for lunch the next day. When Beth said yes, I flew to Philadelphia from Dallas. I didn't tell her I had to be back in Los Angeles that same afternoon to catch the flight to India.

When we arrived at the restaurant, I looked across the table at her and said, "I just wanted to tell you that I have prayed through about this. It's God's will. I love you, and I'm going to marry you."

This is a girl I had never dated. I had never held her hand, never kissed her. She looked at me, smiled sweetly, and said, "You're entitled to your opinion."

"I'm not presuming," I said. "I'm just telling you how I feel. I'm going to be in India for the next three months, and I wanted to let you know that there's an option on the table."

I told Beth I was going to write to her every day. I asked her not to answer my letters. I wanted to write to her and build a foundation of trust. I wanted Beth to know that this was more than chemistry; it was covenant. I wrote to her every day. When I returned to the United States, I flew straight to Philadelphia and sat down with Beth in the same restaurant, at the same table, and asked her the question I'd been waiting to ask for three months: "What do you think?" She smiled and said, "I believe God is in this, and I will marry you."

I could barely contain my excitement. "I don't want to put you under any pressure. Take all the time you need, but ten weeks from today I'm scheduled to be back in India for crusades, and thousands of people are going to get saved in those meetings. If you don't go with me, I'm not going to go, and all those people will die and go to hell. But there's no pressure."

Nine weeks later, December 22, 1976, we were married at First Assembly of God in Wilmington, Delaware. Beth said, "David, my father gave me away the first time. This time I would rather not have him give me away, so when I start down the aisle, will you leave the altar, meet me halfway, and escort me to the altar?"

I said, "I would be delighted." So when Beth started down the aisle, I left the altar to meet her. Folks thought I was leaving the church. I'm sure that after all my years of bachelorhood, the wedding guests thought I had gotten cold feet. We met halfway, and I walked her to the altar. A week later, I walked her down the jetway to a plane bound for India. We had been married for one week when we stepped on the plane.

I had been in India as a single missionary for nine years and didn't know that a widow is considered a curse in Hindu countries. In the Hindu world, a woman's identity only exists in relationship to a man. The most important person in her life is her father. When she applies for a visa, the first question she is asked is her father's name. If she doesn't have a father, she doesn't exist. That is why orphans don't exist. They may live but they are not alive; they have no identity. When a woman marries, the husband takes over the father's role. If the husband dies, the widow loses identity. A woman is always defined in relationship to a man. If she doesn't have a son, she is worthless. Her husband can divorce her because she didn't bear him a son.

Just months after we began to date, Beth and I got married, on December 22, 1976, at First Assembly of God in Wilmington, Delaware.

I had married a widow, and I stood in India in front of ten thousand people and said, "I want to introduce you to my wife, who was a widow." A shock went through the crowd that I never expected. The auditorium exploded. People started saying out loud, "He's married a widow." Y. Jeyaraj, the general superintendent of India, came to me after the service and said, "David, I think it would be best if you never again publicly state that Beth's a widow because in this country being a widow is a curse."

Something inside told me this was an issue where the prevailing norms of a culture were not in line with God's character or with the testimony of Scripture. I asked the superintendent if I might talk about Beth's status with the five hundred pastors I would be speaking to the next morning. He gave me permission. I opened my Bible the next morning and read every scripture about widows and orphans. I began to read the verse where God says, "I am the covering for the widow; I will be her provider, her protector, and her defender. And those who will take advantage of her and the orphan, I will judge them harshly." (See Psalm 68:5 and Deuteronomy 10:18.) Isaiah 54:4–5 says, "You will...remember no more the reproach of your widowhood. For your Maker is your husband— the LORD Almighty is his name—the Holy One of Israel is your Redeemer." Throughout the Old Testament, God says of Himself, "I am the Father of the fatherless." The Father of the fatherless!

Those five hundred pastors fell on their faces and

wept under the conviction of the Holy Spirit. They cried out and said, "The widow will be the most honored person in our church. For God is her covering. God is her defender, her provider, and the orphan we will embrace because He is the Father of the fatherless." God had used Beth's widowhood to show these brothers this part of His character—an insight they would need to release the fullness of the gospel to the Hindu/Muslim world.

More than fifty years in India, and perhaps the best thing I ever did was marry a widow. Then God gave us two daughters who, like us, have a passion for the people of India. Rebecca has a master's degree in theater arts, with a focus on using drama as therapy for abused children. Our daughter Jennifer graduated from Evangel University with a degree in nursing.

Our daughters met Mother Teresa when they were little girls. We were not able to give them a lot of money, but we gave them friendships with some of the greatest people in the world. Our daughters are rich, not in money but in knowing people whose lives have made a difference.

Jennifer volunteered in Mother Teresa's home for the destitute and dying as a student nurse. She had brought latex gloves to wear while working with the diseased and dying women who had been brought off the streets. After the first day, she said, "Dad, I had a decision to make today. I couldn't pray for dying women with latex gloves on my hands. How could I reach out to women so hungry for human touch with sterile gloves?"

I'm so thrilled with my daughters and their hearts for missions, and I owe it all to marrying a widow.

Marrying a widow was not without its challenges. I was thirty-one when Beth and I got married. I had been on my own for fourteen years and traveled constantly during that time. I'm always on the move. Even when I'm home, I can't sit still for long. Like everyone else, my ideas of marriage and family came from my family, and like me, my dad was always on the move, holding revivals while he pastored churches. He wasn't home much. Beth had been in ministry and had been a youth pastor. She had her own ideas about how a family should work. She bore it with amazing grace and patience. But in the late 1980s, matters came to a head. I was flying back and forth to the States almost a couple of times a month, preaching at missions conventions as well as on Speed the Light and Light for the Lost tours. I would fly home for a day or two and then fly out again to the States or to India.

One day Beth sat me down and let me know her concerns. Everything seemed great to me. I had a great wife, two wonderful daughters, and I was doing what God called me to do. Beth informed me that it wasn't great for her or for our girls, who needed a dad for more than one week a month.

I told Beth I would try to do better. Being a middle child had taught me to agree to whatever was being asked. Beth wasn't buying it. She looked at me and told me she wanted a covenant, a written contract that I would agree to and sign. She had drafted what she had in mind. She proceeded to read the document. It began with a string of "Whereases" then moved to "Be it therefore resolved" and a list of things I would do.

I wasn't born last night. I knew this was serious. I listened quietly, felt the sting of conviction, and signed the document. Our covenant has held for more than thirty years. It has proven a durable framework for our life together. Thank God for allowing me to marry a widow who has been willing to challenge me when I needed it.

Beth and I have been blessed with two daughters, Rebecca (left) and Jennifer, who are both serving in ministry with their husbands and children.

It's amazing how time flies. It seems like just yesterday I was holding my daughter Jennifer (top), and here I am holding my grandchildren Gemma Barratt (Jennifer's daughter) and Judah Shults (Rebecca's son).

Beth quickly became the love of my life, the peace in my storms, and the unflappable stability amid my Grant roller coaster of emotions.

Forty-four years of marriage and never a cross word!

Chapter 9

MY INDIAN FAMILY

I CANNOT IMAGINE THE last fifty years without my colleagues in India who have been like family through the years. I've spent more time with them than my natural family. Some, like Pastor Y. Jeyaraj, were fathers or older brothers; others, like David Mohan and Ivan Satyavrata, were as close to me as my brothers.

DAVID MOHAN

David Mohan was a student at Southern Asia Bible College when he and I first met more than fifty years ago. He and his wife, Getzial, were pastoring in Bangalore. Mohan's gifts as a preacher and soulwinner were obvious at a young age. I never doubted that he would build a great church, but what God used him to do exceeded any expectation I had. He has become not only the pastor of the largest Christian church in India but of one of the largest churches in Asia.

Through the years, David Mohan, Beth, and I had the joy of ministering together frequently.

David Mohan is a dear friend whom we helped put through Bible school, and when he graduated, we helped him rent a room, from which he launched his church.

David Mohan planted New Life Assembly of God Church in Chennai (formerly Madras), India, with seven people. Today it has more than sixty thousand members.

David Stewart Sr., a missionary in Chennai (Madras), invited David and Getzial Mohan to come to Madras and start a new church in 1973. I was part of that invitation. A house was rented for David, Getzial, and their son, Samuel. The living room seated about fifteen people. They started New Life Assembly in that room with seven people, including the three of them. Beth and I had the joy of paying the rent the first six months—$30 a month. At the end of six months, Pastor Mohan informed Stewart Sr. that he no longer needed the rent—the church was totally self-supporting.

The church continued to grow. They moved to

a YMCA. The growth of the church outstripped the capacity of any building. The story of New Life reads like the Book of Acts. Healings, deliverances, and dramatic life changes were the norm. It was obvious the Spirit was doing something unusual in Chennai. But New Life was always more than dramatic events; Mohan showed himself to be a strategist of the first order. His approach to cell groups established believers in every neighborhood of the city and in the surrounding suburbs.

For a while they met outdoors and then in various sheds. They prayed for property, but land was ridiculously expensive and almost impossible to obtain. One day a man phoned Mohan and said, "I have one acre available on Mount Road," which is the main street through the heart of Madras, at a cost of $100,000. Mohan immediately asked several people in the church to go with him to view this piece of property. They said to the owner, "We want to buy it. We will buy it. We would like to pray over you and your family and dedicate this property to the Lord." The owner said, "Sure." They prayed over the family and asked for the blessings of God on them. Then they prayed over the property.

Pastor Mohan called me and said, "David, I need $100,000 to buy this property." I made a commitment to help him do this. After making a few phone calls, I sent the $100,000 to Mohan.

Just a few minutes after Mohan and the people

left the property, a local banker drove up and said, "I understand you have this piece of property for sale." The owner said he had just agreed to sell it to Pastor Mohan and New Life Assembly of God. The banker said, "Have you signed any documents?" No binding, legal documents had been signed. The banker asked how much the property had been sold for, and the owner replied, "$100,000." The banker said, "I'll give you $200,000 for the property right now." The owner said, "I'm sorry. That pastor and his people prayed over my family that God would bless us. If I back out now and sell this property to you, their God will curse me. I cannot take that risk." The property was secure. Within days, we had $100,000 in the owner's hands.

That one acre became the site where we built a building to seat twenty-five hundred people. Mohan kept expanding the building until it seated five thousand.

Of course, there were some challenges along the way. The congregation was meeting in a shed at the back of the property that burned down twice. A cyclone came through and blew it down. On another occasion the river flooded it. Four times disasters struck, but Mohan and the people persevered. Then they built the first phase. The church soon reached twenty-five hundred in attendance, and they doubled the size of the auditorium to its present size.

New Life Assembly is the leading church of Southern Asia, with more than sixty thousand members. They have planted hundreds of congregations across India. Mohan has demonstrated that it is possible to build a breakthrough church in a Hindu culture. When Mohan started, few churches had more than fifty or one hundred people. Today's leaders expect great things from God and attempt great things for God. Mohan has been a key part of that development.

I've been asked why Mohan and I became such close friends—more than any other pastor, either in India or the United States. I have no doubt that God put us together all those years ago in Bangalore. We have very similar spirits. Both of us are called to be evangelists. We were both young, enthusiastic, and fervent. We preached together a lot. We were friends from day one. I would invite David to different events in India and overseas. Mohan was quite shy in those days, but I would insist that he come. He is a man of prayer, sincerity, and generosity. There were so many things about him that inspired me and indicated to me, and to others, that this was going to be a great church and he was going to be a great pastor.

Mohan had a beat-up Vespa scooter that was old and constantly broken down. So I applied to Speed the Light (STL), an arm of the US Assemblies of God Youth Ministry that raised money for vehicles, to buy a new scooter for Mohan. STL gave us $800 to help Mohan buy a new scooter. He gave his old Vespa to a pastor who was pioneering a church about fifteen miles away.

I came back to Chennai about a month later and

unexpectedly arrived at his house. The old scooter was sitting out front. When Mohan came to the door, I asked him why he still had the old scooter. He replied, "Oh, Brother Grant, I didn't expect you." I said, "Where's the new scooter?" He said, "I'm sorry I didn't check with you first, but I couldn't give that pioneer pastor my old scooter. It's not reliable, and he's not on a bus route. I'm on a bus route, so I gave him the new scooter and I kept the old one." What could I say? I told him it was perfectly OK. Here was a man who cared more about others than he did for himself. This is exactly why God has blessed him and why so many people have come alongside him. It was never about him; it was always about the work, the kingdom, and how we can help everybody.

More than anyone I have ever known, David Mohan embodies the words of Jesus to His first followers, "Give, and it shall be given unto you; good measure, pressed down, and shaken together, and running over..." (Luke 6:38, KJV). The Lord also said, "It is more blessed to give than to receive" (Acts 20:35), which I think means there is more blessing and more productivity in giving than in receiving. Mohan's life is proof that it's possible to experience incredible blessing regardless of the circumstances.

David Mohan has always been a great man of prayer. He carries the presence of God with him. Years ago, we were spending the night in a hotel room with two single beds. I knelt beside my bed; he knelt beside his bed. We had our prayer time. I stormed heaven and prayed around the world in about fifteen minutes, which is a long time for me to stay in one place. I had prayed around the world and for everybody I could think of, and I crawled into bed. Mohan hadn't said a word in those fifteen minutes. He just knelt there. I didn't say anything. After about half an hour, he uttered one word, "Master." Then total silence. About fifteen minutes later, he uttered the same word again. In forty-five minutes on his knees, Mohan said two words—the same word—"Master." That word was so powerful, and the presence of God was so strong in that room that I lay on my bed and soaked my pillow quietly with tears. It was as if he had such a communion with the Lord that there was no need for words. It was such a beautiful, wonderful, unforgettable moment.

I never spent another night in the same room with Mohan—too much guilt. I often feel the same guilt with Beth, but I manage to get past it. I have to confess that my prayer life has been erratic. As a young teenager, my prayer life was loud, boisterous, passionate, and I would walk and pray for hours— shouting, rejoicing, speaking in tongues, calling on heaven, casting out devils. That was the way my dad prayed, in fact, the way most Pentecostals prayed in my youth. When I got to Calcutta, that was the way Mark Buntain prayed. But for me there was no real intimacy. I was calling down fire from heaven, shouting and filling the prayer room with noise. Then for years

I was alone and prayed silently, and I probably got in a habit of praying without words for many years. And I still, even in sermon preparation, am always thinking about the message, always preparing. I don't sit down for hours and work on a sermon. My feeling is I am looking, looking for how to express the power of God in every situation.

Y. JEYARAJ

My relationship with Y. Jeyaraj was no less important to me than the one with Mohan, though it was different. Jeyaraj was about my father's age and a senior statesman of the church in India. I met Brother Jeyaraj in the early years of my ministry in Tamil Nadu, South India, in the village of Shencottah (Sengottai).

The work in Shencottah had been established by one of the great pioneer missionaries of India, Doris Edwards. "Mother" Edwards, as everyone called her, understood that young people of lower caste had very limited prospects unless they learned a trade. Their place in society was fixed by more than two millennia of law and custom. In that era, college or university was out of the question. The young people of the church would be trapped as day laborers whose very existence was often regarded as an affront to those of high caste. Neither they nor their families would have any opportunity to live above subsistence level. Mother Edwards not only started a church but also founded an industrial training school where more than three hundred children, both boys and girls, received job training each year.

Mother Edwards was a marvelous, godly, strong-willed, powerful, amazing woman who worked in India for fifty-five years. She died and is buried there. You can imagine how strong she had to be. I called her the "steel lady." She had a physical problem that prevented her from lying in a bed to sleep, so she would catnap all day and all night. She would be sitting up and drift off for half an hour or an hour. Then she'd wake up and work. She slept in the car, on the train, and even in church services sometimes.

Even with her health challenges, Mother Edwards proved tireless and incredibly dedicated to the work. She traveled incessantly. She was frugal almost to the point of harshness. She always traveled third class on the train, which must have been torture for her—bare boards that passed for seats, soot and smoke coming in the open windows, no air-conditioning. It was terrible. And yet if there had been a fourth class, she would have traveled in it.

Ernie was no slouch in the frugality department. Speed the Light bought a 1960 Plymouth for Ernie, which he had shipped to India. Ernie could fix anything, and his skills as a mechanic kept that Plymouth on the road for a couple of decades. I don't know how many times I carried auto parts from the US in my luggage. It seems like I went to every junkyard in the

Southeast trying to find carburetors and transmission parts.

Mother Edwards led Jeyaraj to the Lord and became his spiritual mother. For her, discipleship was not a program but a lifestyle, and she infused Jeyaraj with her vision and values. In his twenties, Jeyaraj became her assistant in directing the ministries in Shencottah.

I was traveling across Tamil Nadu preaching in small churches and preached in her little church when I met Jeyaraj. By then he was district superintendent for the State of Tamil Nadu. We became great friends. He encouraged me and translated for me. Jeyaraj treated me with great kindness, and I respected him. He was a powerful man, a fabulous preacher, and a great leader. Jeyaraj was elected general superintendent of South India in the 1970s and later spearheaded the movement to form the All India General Council of the Assemblies of God (later named the General Council of the Assemblies of God of India).

Ninety years ago, in the early days of the Assemblies of God in India, North India and South India were two different worlds. The people of the North and South spoke different languages, and as hard as it is to imagine today, India was a land of hundreds of small states—most with their own language and culture, their own heads of state, even their own foreign ministers. The British were able to dominate by keeping India's people weak and separated.

To a great degree, India was an abstraction until

Gandhi led the independence movement. The subcontinent had never been one country. So not surprisingly, there were two general councils—the General Council of South India and the General Council of North India. In those days, the two councils had more foreign missionaries than national pastors.

In the 1980s, Jeyaraj orchestrated the coming together of these general councils into the All India General Council, which has been a great unifying factor in the eight thousand Assemblies of God churches across India. As the All India General Council's first general superintendent, he left an indelible mark on the Indian church. His oldest son, Robert, carries on this legacy of leadership as he pastors the International Church in Delhi, serves as president of Central Bible College, and heads up Teen Challenge in Delhi.

Like Mohan, Brother Jeyaraj and I traveled a lot together. We would drive to a small village church, often several hours away, hold service, and then turn around and drive home again. Sometimes we drove back and forth to the airport, which was one hundred miles away. It was these hundreds and hundreds of hours traveling together, eating together, and sleeping in the same hotel room that bound us together.

Jeyaraj was a wonderful husband who loved his wife and was unashamed to be openly affectionate—a little unusual in India. They didn't have an arranged marriage in the tradition of their culture but a "love" marriage. She was a Malayali, and he was Tamil, which was not common, but they loved each other dearly.

Jeyaraj looked like my dad, acted like my dad, and carried himself like my dad. He even conducted business meetings like my dad. He had a dominant personality but was a loving man. Everybody wanted him to perform their weddings, to baptize their children, to dedicate their churches. He was tireless. Most nights he slept in the back seat of his car while his driver drove him from one place to the other. He probably had as many nights sleeping in the back seat of his car as he did sleeping in his own bed. He gave himself unsparingly for the church. The Indian church, of all denominations, has produced powerful preachers and leaders, but I think anyone who knew him would say that Y. Jeyaraj was one of the strongest.

Ivan Satyavrata

Ivan Satyavrata may be my most intellectual friend in India and maybe the world, though I would not want to pigeonhole him. Ivan is not just an imposing theological thinker and brilliant lecturer; he is one of the most strategic thinkers in the global body of Christ, a quality that has led to his being appointed to the international board of World Vision.

I met Ivan at Southern Asia Bible College in Bangalore when he was a student. Ivan came from Bombay, where his father worked in the Dutch Consulate. He came from a wonderful but nominally

Christian family. Ivan had gotten involved with some Christian young people in Bombay and gave his life to the Lord. He became a street preacher.

Ivan was considering Bible college, and a friend recommended that he go to Southern Asia Bible College. On her recommendation, he enrolled. He arrived looking like a hippie with his long hair and playing a guitar.

When Ivan saw the campus and its traditional Pentecostal atmosphere, he thought, "What have I gotten myself into?" He determined to leave within a few days. But the president was Dr. John Higgins, a quiet, wonderful man of God who befriended Ivan. Suddenly Ivan was in a dilemma. He didn't like the college and wanted to leave, but the president had become his friend, was kind to him, and encouraged him to stay. Ivan decided to give it a semester, then the rest of the year. One of the faculty members, Dr. Benjamin Shinde, had done the doctor of ministry degree at Fuller Theological Seminary in Pasadena, California. Dr. Shinde had three daughters, and the oldest was a beautiful girl named Sheila. Sometime during that first year, Ivan became interested in Sheila. That kept him at the college.

The Shinde family is Marathi, from the Bombay/Pune area. Ivan's family was from Mangalore (Mangaluru) in Karnataka State, but he had lived in Bombay all his life, which is in Maharashtra State—the Marathi area. That may not seem important to a Westerner, but their backgrounds were altogether different. However, God was in it, and the two got married.

By the time I met Ivan, he had distinguished himself as an outstanding student.

After graduation, Ivan and Sheila enrolled at the Union Biblical Seminary in Pune to do his master's degree. John Higgins had arranged for Ivan to do his studies there with the intent of bringing him back to Southern Asia Bible College as a professor.

I occasionally visited Ivan in Pune. He says that every time they really needed something, I showed up at their door. He graduated and came back to SABC as a new professor. Later the Lord opened doors for Ivan to go to Regent College in Vancouver, British Columbia, to do his master of theology, a degree beyond the master of divinity, and then later to Oxford Centre for Mission Studies in England for his PhD, where his adviser was the eminent British evangelical leader John R. W. Stott. Through all those years in Vancouver and England, I would visit them and, as Ivan says, often when there was a need. It was a privilege to help people like Mohan, Ivan, and others at crucial crossroads of their lives when a little help made all the difference.

Beth and I have been a part of SABC for many years. I have served on the board for almost forty-five years, joyfully raising funds for buildings and scholarships for thousands of ministerial students. Along the way, the school graciously conferred an honorary doctor of divinity degree upon me. Over the years, we've invested more than $2 million in campus construction because we believe so strongly in training students to reach their nations.

I think I inherited Southern Asia Bible College and Continental Theological Seminary in Brussels from Charles Greenaway. He said these were the two schools we should be involved in; we were and still are.

I can't talk about Indian colleagues and omit John Higgins. He and I have been through a lot together over the past forty years. There are few men I respect more than John. The Indian leaders love him, and he could have been president of SABC for life, but John felt the time had come to turn the school over to Indian leadership. He stepped aside, continued to be a professor there, and brought in Dr. A. C. George, who had been a professor at the college, to be the first national president. When A. C. George retired, Ivan was named president, a title he carried with consummate skill and authority. When John retired from leadership in Calcutta, he nominated Ivan to be the leader of Assemblies of God ministries in the city, a huge responsibility that includes a church of four thousand people, ten congregations in one building, one hundred satellite churches, schools with more than thirty thousand children, a hospital, and a nursing school. Ivan and I have been close from his days as a student to the present.

Ivan Satyavrata of Southern Asia Bible College (SABC), shown here with his wife, Sheila Shinde, would later become president of SABC and senior pastor of the Assemblies of God church in Calcutta. We're so blessed to call them friends.

Because of the closeness of our families, Ivan and Sheila adopted Rebecca when she lived in Calcutta. Families in India become involved with others. If your friend's child is in your city, you open your doors and expect the child to stay with you. When your child is in their city, they expect your child to stay with them. They look after your child as if the child is theirs. When Rebecca arrived in India, the Satyavratas said, "Our daughter has arrived; David Grant's daughter is here; family is here." They not only provided a bed for Rebecca, they also protected her, mentored and guided her, and told her exactly what to do with her life. It's a wonderful relationship that continues to this day. This is not the exception; it's the rule. Mother Edwards adopted all five of Jeyaraj's children and sent them to the States for college. Beth and I have done the same when the children of other leaders have come to the US for study or ministry.

I have spent a lifetime with my Indian colleagues. We have walked together; spent time together; preached together; prayed, eaten, and traveled together; and encouraged each other. Because of that, we have a level of trust and shared life that has carried us through a lot of crises. I've sometimes been accused of being "too close" to the Indian church and its leaders and always taking "their side." I don't understand how I can be "too close" to the people God called me to serve or to my adopted nation. Jesus called twelve to be with Him. They lived together, traveled together, ate together, slept together, laughed together, and wept together. Jesus even washed their feet, which sounds way "too close."

Chapter 10

NO PROBLEM

I NEVER FELT I was especially talented or gifted, but one quality that has helped me is that I believe there's always a way to get where I'm going. I don't believe in dead ends. For me, life is more like a maze. When one pathway closes, I keep going until I find a way through.

Our Indian colleagues have a similar approach to life. When a situation gets complicated, they will look at me and say, "No problem, Brother David." They don't mean there is no problem or that the problem is inconsequential; they mean they will find a way to work through it. That's one more reason we have worked so well together.

Anyone who knows me knows I have trouble sitting still. It doesn't matter where I am or what's going on; I'm happiest when I'm in a crowd or in motion—or, better yet, when I am in motion in a crowd. That's why being sidelined is a challenge. When the coronavirus pandemic upended life in America and around the world in 2020, causing businesses, churches, and schools to close, I had friends who talked about getting sabbatical time, the joy of slowing down, and taking it easy. I was not rejoicing; I was chafing.

Beth and I worked out of Brussels throughout the 1980s. It was a perfect location given our commitments in India and the schedule of missions conventions and tours in the States. Our regional director, Charles Greenaway, wanted us there. He wanted us to help foster the growth and development of Continental Theological Seminary in Brussels. We were glad to help in any way we could.

When Greenaway retired, the regional director for Southern Asia was promoted to take his place. He had a different approach to the job, which is not surprising because there was only one Charles Greenaway. The new director wanted me to travel less and stay overseas, which would mean raising fewer funds. As a middle child, I learned to go with the flow and be a team player, so I was ready to do what he asked.

The day after the new director gave me the news, I was in Dallas for a convention when I ran into Charles Greenaway in the lobby of the hotel. He looked at me and said, "Boy, what's the matter with you? Is middle management trying to clip your wings?" Charles had been retired for several years and no longer lived in Springfield, but it was obvious to him, and anyone who knew me, that something was wrong. The bounce was gone out of my step. In classic Greenaway style, he went on, glowering like a boxing manager between rounds and punching the air with his right fist. "Don't ever apologize for your God-given strengths," he said. "Be yourself." Greenaway had been a second father to me for years but never more than on that morning, and he was more exercised than I was. I was at peace with whatever direction God had for us.

Twenty minutes later, Executive Director Phil Hogan pulled me aside. "I hear middle management is trying to clip your wings." Either Greenaway or the Holy Spirit had gotten to Hogan in the interim. I was betting on Greenaway. "Move back to the States. You'll answer to me." In less than ten words Hogan had solved a problem. And there, in microcosm, was what made J. Philip Hogan a great leader. He knew his people. He could quickly assess a situation, make a decision, and stick to his guns. Phil Hogan never responded to a survey with "No opinion." As the years have passed, it's become clear that this shift opened doors that neither Beth nor I ever imagined.

A few weeks later, Dr. John Higgins called. John had been the dean at Southern Asia Bible College in Bangalore but had recently been named dean at Southeastern. He asked Beth to join the faculty as Missionary-in-Residence. She would teach full-time, and I would work out of Lakeland. It seemed perfect.

Beth blossomed in her new role. The regimen of focused reading, lecture preparation, and interacting with students brought out her best. John soon talked to Beth about getting her doctorate, and the seed was planted that led her to Biola University and earning a PhD in Intercultural Education. The doctorate opened doors in our fellowship and around the world. It has given Beth credibility and entree into the halls of government as well as academia.

John Higgins even asked me to teach. I had seventy-five freshmen in an evangelism class. Thirty missionaries came out of that one class, including Joe and Laurie Gordon and Doug and Ramona Jacobs, who have served in Southern Asia for almost twenty-five years. I would never have chosen to base out of Lakeland, Florida, but it set the stage for the second half of our ministry.

Mark Buntain died suddenly in 1989, leaving a huge loss in every way. Mark was the beating heart of the Calcutta mission. His compassion, energy, and determination had set the agenda for the ministry for thirty-five years. Mark had also been the face of India and the face of compassion ministry in the States for years.

Mark Buntain was an apostle. He did more in Calcutta in thirty-five years than any mission agency or denomination had done in almost two hundred years. He built one of the strongest Pentecostal churches in India, started forty-three churches and schools, fed as many as fifty thousand people a day, built a hospital, and started a nursing school. Given his calling, personality, and the fact that he was the son of a general superintendent of the Pentecostal Assemblies of Canada, a certain amount of tension with leadership was inevitable. Mark knew who he was and where he was going—and he was determined to get there.

Huldah, Mark's widow, was as strong-willed as he was. She saw the Calcutta mission as something she and Mark had built. Like Mark, she would do what she believed God wanted her to do, without outside interference. The situation was complicated by the fact that Mark had worked with a group of leading pastors to establish the Calcutta Mission of Mercy, a quasi-independent organization to raise money for Calcutta. Because of who those pastors were, Mark had leverage that few other missionaries had. That board was loyal to Mark and saw themselves as custodians of the vision. Huldah was also getting to the place that she needed assistance.

The US Assemblies of God leader responsible for India asked me to become the area director to coordinate our efforts in the area and to help with the transition in Calcutta. I said, "No. I know where my strengths lie, and administration is not one of them."

I loved Mark and Huldah like family and wanted to see the mission continue to reach the broken and hurting in Calcutta, but I knew some transition would be necessary. I was committed to doing it in a way that honored God as well as Mark and Huldah.

The regional director asked me to go to Calcutta to assess the situation and make recommendations. I spent five weeks there on the most challenging assignment of my career. I met with Huldah and her staff. I spent hours with John Higgins, who had left Southeastern University to return to India and was now pastoring the Calcutta church. After five weeks and dozens of meetings, it was obvious to me that it was time for a change in leadership.

I've watched this scenario play out in churches, universities, denominations, and missions. Great leaders get near the end and can't see when the time has come for them to step aside. I knew we would need God's help to transition in a way that would not compromise all that Mark and Huldah had worked so hard to accomplish.

I will always be thankful for Thomas E. Trask, the general superintendent of the Assemblies of God who chaired the meeting where the decision was made that Huldah would retire. He showed great patience and compassion. Two things came out of that meeting: Huldah was allowed to retire from her role as leader of the ministry, which she did with dignity and grace; and, most important, the Calcutta mission was preserved and placed on the road to a new season of impact and effectiveness. It took a decade to get there, but today the ministries are stronger, more vibrant, and healthier than ever. The mission is led by Dr. Ivan Satyavrata, who has gained a level of international respect and influence for Calcutta that could never have occurred under a foreigner. Mark would be proud.

Huldah Buntain (far left), senior pastor of the Calcutta Assemblies of God (AG) church, is shown here at one of its many memorable Sunday services. She is on the platform with Jerry Parsley, Eurasia regional director of AG World Missions (center), and me.

Beth, baby Rebecca, and I are shown here at one of Mark and Huldah Buntain's ever-welcoming Sunday dinners at 2/C Camac Street in Calcutta.

Beth, baby Rebecca, and I are at a Bible school graduation in Kerala, South India, with missionary Phyllis Sorbo. This was one of more than two hundred graduations for ministry students we participated in over the course of fifty years.

Chapter 11

GOD OF THE FATHERLESS

S INCE MY YOUTH in Pensacola, I've had a deep appreciation for Teen Challenge. In centers around the world, Teen Challenge has been used by God to salvage the lives of tens of thousands of young people who would have otherwise had no hope. So when we had the opportunity to partner with K. K. Devaraj to launch a Teen Challenge Center in Bombay (now Mumbai) for the three hundred thousand street kids of the city, we threw ourselves into the project. I stopped by almost every time I went to India.

Devaraj is not a typical preacher. After graduating from university with a degree in engineering, he went to Iran to work in the oil fields. While there, he accepted Christ as His Savior. When radical Shiites overturned the Shah's government in 1979, Devaraj left Iran and went to Beirut, where he encountered the work of Teen Challenge. God spoke to Devaraj and told him to return to India and start a Teen Challenge Center in Bombay.

Devaraj combines the analytical ability of an engineer with the entrepreneurial spirit of a captain of industry. He's always looking for creative ways to reach and rescue the most vulnerable. After several years of reaching out to street kids and drug addicts, Devaraj and his staff discovered that one hundred thousand little girls had been sold into prostitution in the red-light district of Bombay. Suddenly and unexpectedly, he found himself in the sordid world of sex trafficking.

More than one million girls have been sold or kidnapped into prostitution in India, Nepal, Bangladesh, and Sri Lanka. Sex trafficking is more than a social problem in Southern Asia; it is a global scandal. Girls from Russia and Ukraine fill the brothels of Western Europe and the United States. Experts estimate that ten million girls in two hundred nations have been sold into prostitution. Pimps from all over the world buy and sell little girls and women. Prostitution has become the new slavery. Millions of women and girls, as well as young men and boys, live in bondage, terror, and torture.

When we discovered those one hundred thousand girls in the red-light district of Bombay, we had a street meeting, and one hundred young prostitutes gave their hearts to Jesus. But they could not leave the brothels because each one had been sold for about $200 by their parents, and none of them had the money to repay the pimps who had bought them.

It's hard for us to fathom sex trafficking. These girls have been sold into slavery by their own parents. Their fathers sold them to be raped, beaten, and brutalized. The typical prostituted woman or child in Bombay's red-light district may be raped by as many as twenty men a day and dies of AIDS by the time she is twenty-one. Those girls could not leave the brothels, but they asked our Teen Challenge workers to take their daughters to a place of safety. They gave us thirty-seven little girls one night, most of them born in the brothel. We opened our first Home of Hope in Bombay for those thirty-seven little girls. Six months later, we had over one hundred.

A madam in one of the brothels came to Jesus. She led every girl in her brothel to Christ within just a few weeks. She then sold us the building for $5,000, and we put a church in it. In the midst of all that horror and depravity, we now had a center where the victims of sex trafficking could be rescued and restored.

I remember when another madam called us and said, "You're taking little babies, little girls, in your Home of Hope in Bombay. Here's a three-year-old that you can have. Her nineteen-year-old mother died yesterday of AIDS. The child was born with AIDS. She's going to die. You can have her."

One of our wonderful Spirit-filled doctors treated

the children every week. He phoned me six months after we opened the Home of Hope and said, "David, you'd better sit down because I'm going to tell you a story that I can hardly believe myself. In my thirty years of medical practice, I have seen many miracles, but the one I saw today is the best."

The doctor continued, "You know I go every week and treat the children at the Home of Hope. A three-year-old with AIDS was given to us six months ago, and I have tested her every week. I tested her today, and there's not a trace of the AIDS virus in her body. God has stretched out His hand and healed that little girl. I don't understand it, but God has done something that we cannot understand."

Today we have twelve Homes of Hope and ministries in twenty cities. Those ministry teams help more than fifty thousand women and girls each year. We started by rescuing the children of trafficked women, then the young girls, and now women. Madams have come to Christ. The ministry has expanded to every country in Southern Asia, to Africa, and to Europe. Why? Because God is not willing that one of those girls should perish.

I have a dream that I will stand at the door at the marriage supper of the Lamb and say, "Welcome to Father's house. In Father's house you cannot be sold. You cannot be abused. You will never be betrayed." The image of Father's house has seized me in recent years. There is room for everybody in Father's house.

It doesn't matter who you are or what you've done or what has been done to you. There is room for you there.

I want to walk you through Bombay's red-light district. The busiest time is midnight. The streets are jammed with thousands of men. I want to walk you by the little girls that are standing on the street corners, dressed provocatively, inviting men to rape them. When you get close enough, you see that their eyes are dead. They're smiling, but their eyes are dead. Their hearts are like stone.

Now I want to take you to the Home of Hope and introduce you to little girls whose eyes are dancing, whose hearts are once again hearts of flesh. Because Isaiah 61 says, "[He will] bestow on them a crown of beauty instead of ashes, the oil of joy instead of mourning, and a garment of praise instead of a spirit of despair."

A nineteen-year-old girl stood up one day and testified, "My father sold me for $200 when I was twelve years old. For seven years I was in prostitution. Now God has rescued me and made me a new creature in Christ Jesus. He has washed my blood, and washed my memories, and I am brand new. I have scars on my body, but not on my heart." Three years later, I stood at the altar when she married a young man out of our Teen Challenge program. That couple are now two of our most effective ministers in Bombay. God reached down and gave them resurrection and new beginnings.

That reminds me of one of the challenges we've faced

in Bombay because so many young ladies are healed and restored. As God puts their lives back together, many of them get married. In one year alone we had twenty-five weddings! We needed to buy twenty-five wedding gowns. A supporter of the ministry from Toronto bought almost all of them. What a wonderful problem to have.

My daughter Rebecca called me while she was ministering in the brothels in India and said, "Dad, one eleven-year-old girl told me about her rape and the brutality, the horror, she went through. I couldn't sleep last night; I had nightmares all night long."

I said, "Becca, you've got to spend time in prayer because if you just give yourself to the girls all the time, you will run out of anything to give. You've got to put margins in your life." Here I was talking to my own daughter about margins I didn't have.

They brought a seven-year-old girl off the street in Calcutta. Her mother, who was a prostitute, had died. She never knew her father, just one of the thousands of men who had visited her mother, but she had found Jesus. They brought her into our home because she had no family. The doctor examined her and said, "Seven years in a brothel. She's not going to make it." She was nothing but skin and bones; her arms and legs were not much bigger than my finger, but she knew Jesus. She became like my adopted niece. Every free moment she would sit beside me. We often went to church together. When it came time for me to leave India, I put my arms around her and said, "Uncle David's got to go back to America. I'll see you in a few weeks."

She said, "No, Uncle David, I won't be here when you come back." She knew she was dying. She knew she had no future. I started to say something, but I couldn't; my throat closed. I couldn't speak. Tears began to run down my face. She took her tiny hand and brushed the tears off my face and preached the greatest sermon I have ever heard.

"Don't worry about me, Uncle David. I've got Jesus, and He's all I need." Seven years old, no father, no mother, no future, a dying little girl out of a brothel in Calcutta, but she had Jesus. I couldn't speak. I hugged her, put her back on the floor, and stumbled out of the house crying.

I was still crying when the plane took off from Calcutta. I said, "Lord, there's a million children on those streets, but there's a seven-year-old girl down there, and she's dying. She doesn't have a father or a mother or a future, but she says, 'I've got Jesus, and He's all I need.'"

Every church I went to, I shared her story. I asked people to pray for that dying girl. A few months later I flew back to Calcutta, stepped out of the airport, and that little girl came screaming down the sidewalk, "Uncle David, Uncle David!" I swept her up in my arms and said the stupidest thing I've ever said. I said, "Honey, what are you doing here?" I wish I'd had the faith for her healing, but I did not.

She looked at me and said matter-of-factly, "Uncle David, Jesus has healed me. I'm perfectly normal. I told you, I've got Jesus. And I have a new mother and a new father. I've been adopted by a Christian family and, Uncle David, I've got a father. For the first time in my life, I have a father." I stood there holding the little girl. She had gained twenty pounds. She had passed her eighth birthday. She was no longer dying, and she was no longer an orphan. Why? Because God is the Father of the fatherless.

God has given me the opportunity to minister on thousands of platforms in thousands of places around the world. On the street, in churches, in red-light districts, the message of Jesus and His power to save is the same.

Chapter 12

EXCLUDED

I'VE BEEN BLESSED with great favor from God and governments over my fifty years of ministry on the Indian subcontinent. Over time there is a tendency to grow comfortable and to take that favor for granted. That came to a screeching halt one day when I arrived at the airport in Chennai (Madras) and the customs official told me I could not enter the country.

I always knew that the door to India could close. When I was in Bible school, some missionaries would talk about closed doors and the urgency of working "while it is yet day." But I never talked about closed doors. It ran contrary to my optimistic nature. I'd rather talk about open doors and opportunity. Still, the possibility that I could be refused entry to India was always there. I lived as if every trip to India might be my last, and I determined to make every moment count.

My mind raced through a dozen scenarios. Had something appeared in our quarterly newspaper, *Today's India*, that found its way into the hands of an unfriendly government official? Was it connected to Project Rescue, our ministry to victims of human trafficking? Did an angry leader or a disgruntled employee work a contact in the system to exclude us?

When you serve as area director with leadership responsibility for one hundred American team members and several thousand national churches, conflict is inevitable. Loren Triplett, a longtime executive director of Assemblies of God World Ministries, used to say, "Missionaries are a lot like manure. They're only good when they're spread out. They smell in a pile." I am sure Loren was right. Sometimes missionaries argue with each other. At other times, conflict flares between missionaries and national leaders. Battles occur from time to time when missionaries forget they are always guests in the host country. Sometimes national leaders fight with each other. Conflict, anywhere and anytime, engenders deep feelings. That comes as a shock to many believers in the States. But conflict is a fact of life and of church.

The New Testament preserves the history of conflict in the churches of the first century, between leaders and in the churches. I get amused when people talk about restoring the New Testament church. Conflict was part of the New Testament church, and it wasn't all bad. The first conflict between the Palestinian Jewish believers and the Greek Jews resulted in a more efficient daily distribution of bread to widows in the Jerusalem church. The conflict over how Jewish followers of Jesus were to treat Gentile believers resulted in the first church council and the removal of barriers to membership in the community. The decisions of that council made Christianity more open to people of all ethnic backgrounds and provided a launching pad for the global growth of Christianity. So conflict was not always bad; sometimes it propelled the church toward new models of ministry and greater effectiveness.

Conflict can also be destructive when it boils over and people do things that are detrimental to others and to the cause of Christ. A leadership conflict within the Indian church spilled over to the government when someone in the church there filed a formal protest with the Home Ministry in New Delhi, which oversees visas.

On that trip to Chennai, I walked to immigration as I had a hundred times in the past thirty years. The immigration official punched in my passport number, and what he saw on the computer screen caused his facial expression to change visibly. He said, "Just a moment," and immediately went into the supervisor's office. I'm very sensitive to what's going on in moments like this, so I looked around the corner at his computer and read my name. It stated, "David Grant should not be allowed to enter India. There has been a complaint filed against him. Though he has a valid visa, he is to be refused entry and he's not to be informed of the reason."

I was speed-reading through this message. When the officer returned with his supervisor, the supervisor invited me into his office and said, "Mr. Grant, I'm so sorry because we are friends with your friends that you're coming to visit here, but we have instructions from Delhi that you are not to be allowed to enter the country. We have to put you back on British Airways and back to London."

I assured the supervisor that I fully understood his dilemma. I said, "I've been anticipating this for some time because there are some conflicts that I'm in the middle of, and someone has unfortunately taken the conflict to another level. It's not your fault."

He seemed relieved. I was back on British Airways and headed for London within an hour. There was a lot of consternation, disappointment, and confusion for my family and friends while I was on the flight from Madras to London. David Stewart Sr., the local Assemblies of God World Ministries leader in Chennai, phoned my wife and said he was sorry to inform her that I was not allowed to land. He also said that he had phoned Springfield, Missouri, and the executives knew. They were all concerned at how disappointed and upset I would be, but I was sound asleep with a very restful, peaceful spirit. This was something I had anticipated for thirty years. Now that it had occurred, I would deal with it.

When I landed in London, I immediately called Beth. She asked how I felt. I said, "Great. I just had nine solid hours of sleep." Usually, I don't sleep on planes very well, but this time I did. I told her I was changing my ticket and flying to Washington, DC, and would go to the Indian Consulate the next morning to start working on the problem. It has never been my nature to sit and wait for things to happen. Now was the time to draw on thirty years of relationships to fix the problem.

I phoned our regional director and informed him I would be in Washington at the Indian Embassy the next day. So began one of the most fascinating chapters of my life, a chapter that I look on as miraculous, amazing, and heartwarming. My friends in India immediately went to work to reverse the decision and get my name off the blacklist. They worked with their friends in the government in India. I worked with friends in the Indian Embassy. The Lord gave us favor, wonderful favor. Normally, in a situation like this, the government decision is never reversed. This time, there was amazing flexibility. Embassy staff assured me that they appreciated the work we were doing in their country. We talked about who may have filed the complaint, why the government considered the complaint, and how to change the result. The embassy staff

behaved as friends and not merely government func-
tionaries. I will always be grateful to them.

I told the staff there was an important leadership
meeting coming up in India, and it would be good if
I could attend. They offered me a ninety-day, single-
entry visa. My friends said, "When you go to India, fly
from Singapore to Bangalore because there are no com-
puters yet at immigration in that airport." Everything
was supposed to be very confidential. No one was to
know I was coming so that whoever had complained
would not have the opportunity to frustrate the process. There were a few within our national church who
would have preferred that I never return to India again.
But Indian church leaders and the wonderful national
friends were absolutely committed to reversing this
process.

We decided that Beth would go to India two days
before I did to be part of the leadership meeting and
that she and I would not be on the same plane. I
would arrive in the middle of the meeting. I flew from
Singapore to Bangalore as planned. My friends in India
had said, "Make sure you get a seat in the first row so
that when you land in Bangalore, they will know how
to identify you."

When I landed in Bangalore, two government offi-
cials boarded the aircraft and said to me, "Are you
David Grant?"

I said, "Yes, I am."

They said, "Come with us."

They escorted me off the plane, through immigration—they had taken care of all the formalities—through baggage claim, and told me not to worry about the baggage. They said they would have it brought out to me. No one was supposed to know I was coming. It was to be totally confidential. The immigration officers escorted me through customs and into the reception hall and said, "Your friends are waiting for you."

Thirty people had gathered to welcome me home. Highly confidential? Top secret? No one was supposed to know! But there stood the district superintendent, the president of the local Bible college, spouses, and dear colleagues. They were crying, and I was too. As we embraced, laughed, and cried, they said, "What a wonderful thing the government has allowed us to do. God has given us favor."

The Indian leaders immediately drove me to the leadership meeting, where some were happy and some unpleasantly surprised. Several leaders were definitely not happy to see me. I'm sure a few had been thrilled that I would never be able to enter India again. The conflict had been intense. The moment reminded me of the story from Acts when Peter appeared at the gate and no one believed it was Peter, even though they had prayed for his release. When I walked into the room where the leaders were meeting, it was amazing. Friends leapt to their feet with surprise and not a few tears, because Beth had not told them I might be able to get in. We embraced with relief and thanksgiving to God. Just a few were less than enthusiastic, but that was OK too.

The process of restoring my visa was miraculous. I will never forget the government official who looked at me and said, "I am the one who placed your name on the blacklist, and I'll be the one to take it off." There were actually four blacklists in four separate agencies. The official took a personal political risk to remove my name from all four. He not only removed my name from the blacklists, he issued me a new ten-year visa. It was an unlikely and wonderful turn of events.

Those who sought to cause difficulties stepped back from the conflict, at least for a time. The controversy abated. What remains is a deep sense of family—people who would lay down their lives for each other. So the story of the lost visa is also the story of powerful, deep relationships that transcend ordinary life and move you into the realm of the Book of Acts.

The lost visa stands out in my heart and mind as a difficult, painful time. But as Joseph said when he was reunited with the brothers who sold him years earlier into slavery, "You intended to harm me, but God intended it for good" (Gen. 50:20). This is what I call a conversion of circumstances, when God allows something difficult to happen so that He can get a greater glory out of it. And a greater glory was accomplished as our relationship to the Indian church went deeper than ever. It was a reminder that God is still over all and very much aware of what transpires inside and outside the church.

God has miraculously opened doors for me to preach throughout India, even in the face of what seemed to be insurmountable odds. From age five to seventy-five, preaching has been my passion and joy.

Chapter 13

ACCUSED

THEY SAY THAT hope springs eternal. It certainly does for me. I don't think I've ever had a completely negative day in my life. I always try to see the best in people and in situations. When we got through the visa problem, I hoped, and believed, that the situation would improve. It did in the sense that my relationships with the Indian leaders reached a new depth. But as much as I hate to admit it, my good friend Ron Maddux is right when he says, "People can change but not much." Years later, two missionaries who lacked extensive experience in India and who did not have deep relationships with Indian leaders accused me of bribing my way back into India.

They were people who lived offended. I never thought that was a good way to live. I believe the gospel results in a lifestyle of "un-offendedness." I have chosen not to be offended. Offense is like a cancer. It will kill you. I know a number of people who died of offense. The death certificate may have listed the cause as "cancer," "stroke," or something else, but their lifestyle of offense had robbed them of life.

The apostle Paul warned believers, "Neither give place to the devil" (Eph. 4:27, KJV). Offense and bitterness give the enemy a foothold in a person's heart and a passageway into their innermost being. I have made up my mind not to give the devil a toll pass to my heart. Some of my colleagues, who had been offended for years, put the worst possible construction on a relationship that God had provided to help us and allowed an official to come closer to Jesus.

The embassy official in Washington who had been so gracious in helping me with my visa problem had a son enrolled in an American college and was struggling to pay his school expenses. The official said, "I know you are an educator and you're helping a lot of young people go to school and college. You scholarship a lot of these students. Is there any way you can help my son?" So we helped with a scholarship for his son. In the meantime, I was regularly going to the official's home to pray with his family. He expressed a desire to work for Project Rescue when he retired.

I had lived and worked with the Indian leaders for thirty years. We had grown up in the ministry together. We traveled together, ate together, and roomed together. We walked in covenant relationships of mutual accountability. So I talked to my Indian brothers and told them everything and asked them to judge the situation. I told them I would submit to their wisdom. They were comfortable with my relationship with the official and thankful that God had opened a door of influence with such a strategically placed person. I talked with our senior American colleagues in India—leaders who had given their lives to India—and they were comfortable. The accusers would not see anything in a positive light. They could only see the situation through the lenses of their offense.

So I had to face their accusations. The executive leaders of the Assemblies of God, to whom I have been accountable throughout my ministry, were brought together to judge the validity of the accusations. It was one of the hardest days of my life.

I will never forget Dr. Trask's response to the allegations when one of my lifelong friends called him on my behalf to express his concern. Dr. Trask told him, "David will be fine. He will emerge from this without the smell of smoke on his clothes." By God's mercy and through discerning leaders, I was cleared of all accusations.

The conflict in India took a new and bizarre turn in 2013. In September, I was in Calicut to speak at the national leadership meeting. Unknown to me, a dissident group who had seceded from the Assemblies of God were looking for a way to embarrass the national leadership. They bribed a police officer to arrest me on charges of preaching without the proper visa. I had been going there for fifty years on the same type of visa. I had preached thousands of times in outdoor meetings, churches, and schools. I had never been accused of breaking the law.

The man took the bribe. Before the end of the leadership meeting, two policemen came to my hotel to interview me. They said, "You are preaching without the proper visa." I responded that for fifty years I had been careful to follow the regulations, and I felt comfortable with the visa situation. I also informed them that I knew who had sent them. They left without going any further.

After the meeting, the dissidents went back to the policeman and demanded he do something. He filed a false report that stated he had arrested me, and I had escaped.

In a matter of hours, Pastor Mohan saw a report on the news that David Grant had been arrested, escaped, and was now a fugitive from justice. Mohan urged me to get on a plane and fly out of the country. I did exactly what he told me to do.

I came back to India six months later for scheduled leadership meetings. As soon as I got off the plane in Delhi, I was arrested and taken to court. A female judge was deeply offended by the disgraceful treatment of a female Indian diplomat who had been arrested and strip-searched by the New York police. Normally, an arraignment in India is quick, bail is set, and the accused is on the street in a couple of hours. The judge was not having it. She stated that no bail would be set. Instead of being on the street in a couple of hours, I was on my way to Tihar, India's most notorious prison, which has more than twelve thousand inmates.

I was placed in a cell with seventy other men. Some of them were young, others were advanced in years. Some had the faces of men who had committed a thousand sins; others were sullen. All had the look of having been ground down by life. It was a place of hopelessness and despair. I thought of Paul and Silas in prison, and I determined that if they could bring the presence of God into a Roman jail, I could bring the presence of God into an Indian prison.

I made friends with a number of the inmates. They understood why they were there; they could not understand why I, "a rich American," was there. I never thought of myself as rich, but I suddenly was aware that to prisoners in an Indian jail I looked rich in my blue blazer, gray flannel slacks, and blue shirt. "Surely," they said, "you could bribe someone. Why are you here?" I told them I was accused of preaching on the wrong visa. One of them said, "You are a preacher? Will you pray for us?"

Before I knew it, a prayer line formed and I was laying hands on hardened criminals. Several of them invited Jesus to come into their hearts and change their lives. I thought about the incredible, determined love of God. God loved those men so much that He sent me to jail to bring them into His family.

Despite my joy at what God was doing in the prison, I was in serious trouble. If found guilty, I could receive a five-year sentence. Beth was already planning to find an apartment in Calicut to be close to me in prison if I could not get bail. Miraculously, I had the peace of God from the moment they took me into custody. I somehow knew that God was at work in whatever was happening.

Our Indian church family worked almost around the clock with Beth. The hotel where Beth and our son-in-law, Jonathan, stayed was filled with our friends. Mohan and Devaraj were the first to arrive. By the time the police took me to the courtroom, Y. Jeyaraj's son, Robert, had arrived. Ivan and Sheila Satyavrata came soon thereafter. Friends in India and around the world prayed. A lady in New York City sent a check for $30,000 to pay the legal expenses.

After four days in Tihar prison, I appeared before the judge in New Delhi, who released me to the custody of the arresting officer, who would return me to Calicut for my court appearance there. God had touched the man's heart. He told the judge I should be released to his custody and housed in a hotel where two officers would stand outside my door twenty-four hours a day while we waited for the hearing. He said, "You can trust this man not to run." The same policeman who had taken a bribe to arrest me now became my advocate and worked behind the scenes on my behalf.

The judge deliberated for four days. The offense was non-bailable, but after four days, with thousands of believers praying, the judge miraculously granted bail. Two believers from Calicut whom I didn't even know posted my bail by pledging their homes. The judge told me I was free to go anywhere I wanted, including the US, so long as I pledged to come back for the trial.

The legal process dragged on for more than a year, and then the judge dismissed the case. All the witnesses for the prosecution had become hostile to the prosecution. It was clear to me that God had gone before us.

We saw a miracle beyond the revival in Tihar prison: a revival of unity in the Indian church. Our Indian family had come together. They were ashamed of what the dissidents had done and the shame they had brought on the Indian church. They drew closer to each other and distanced themselves from the dissidents. We were thankful for the positive outcomes, all of them, and especially for those men in the prison who discovered the God who loves them and died for them.

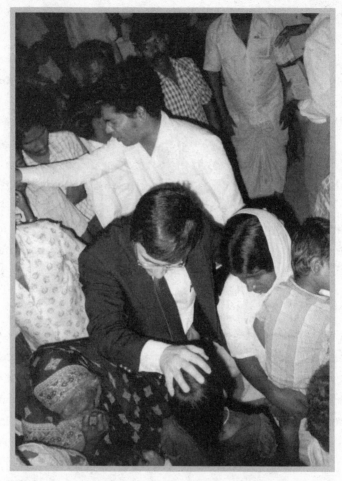

When Jesus saw the masses, He had compassion and healed them. I'm always moved by the immensity of need and people desperate for Him.

I was born to give in the land God called me to as a twelve-year-old boy when I put my life in the offering pan.

Chapter 14

NEXT GENERATION

O NE OF THE highlights of my life came just before the 2019 General Council meeting of the Assemblies of God in Orlando, Florida, when Beth and I were honored with the Influencer Lifetime Achievement Award for our contributions to our fellowship. In addition to co-founding and directing Project Rescue, Beth has published a groundbreaking text on the theology of compassion, been a university professor, and is the first woman to be elected to our parent fellowship's Executive Presbytery in the more than one-hundred-year history of the organization. Many of Beth's greatest contributions have been like her: quiet, understated, and unobtrusive. Her insight, wisdom, and patience have been a blessing to every committee and task force on which she has served. Beth has carved out a legacy of leadership and influence that has opened doors for women in ministry here and around the world. She has encouraged thousands of young women to pursue their callings and to believe God to help them overcome any barriers in their way.

The conference leaders asked Beth to share with the audience, which included over a thousand next-generation leaders. Rather than address her remarks to our generation, Beth spoke to those young leaders, challenging them to confront the darkness in our world with hope, faith, and commitment. She preached the sermon of a lifetime, though it might be better to say that she delivered her lifetime message. Hundreds of young people responded to her appeal to give their lives to service.

As I stood next to Beth on that platform and we both looked out at the tear-stained faces of the next generation, we felt like we were passing the torch to them. It's something we've been working on for more than forty years, but it became a major focus of ministry as we moved into our seventies and dealt with the physical challenges of aging. We've been raising up leaders our whole ministry. This is why we have invested so heavily in Bible schools. We saw training and equipping tomorrow's leaders today as our primary calling. The thousands of young people we have "scholarshipped" to Bible colleges were our succession plan. They would carry the gospel to the unreached peoples of our region. We never had an organization that we felt compelled to perpetuate.

Project Rescue created a new wrinkle in the plan. For the first time in our life together, we built a ministry organization that included feeding the hungry and resourcing schools for trafficked women and children. The ministry to trafficked women and children in Mumbai (Bombay) has spread to cities across Southern Asia, Africa, and Europe. We raise funds to staff our Homes of Hope, train and deploy the workers, fund outreaches, and support the young women and men God has helped us rescue and restore—more than fifty-one thousand in 2020 alone.

Somebody has to coordinate and direct that effort.

As we have seen for over forty years, God always has a plan, and that plan centers on His people. God has given us a team of young women and men with a passion for the lost and broken. It started with our two daughters, Rebecca and Jennifer, who were teenagers when we first visited the brothels of Mumbai with Devaraj. We started Project Rescue when Rebecca was sixteen and Jennifer was twelve. In a sense, they grew up with this ministry. They met girls their age and even younger whose lives had been destroyed by sex trafficking. They could see themselves in the faces of the girls in our Mumbai Home of Hope. They became friends and, eventually, sisters to each of them. Year by year, the seeds planted in their young hearts grew into God's vision for their lives.

By the time Rebecca and Jennifer graduated high school, they were already thinking about where they fit in God's rescue project for trafficked women and children. Neither Beth nor I ever tried to push them in that direction. We knew they would be storming the very gates of hell, and hell would fire back. Only the call of God on their lives could sustain them in that work, and we knew, if we called them to the work, we would have to work to keep them there. I had seen too many clergy do that to their kids. We would not do that to Rebecca and Jennifer.

Rebecca studied drama and speech education at Evangel University and later earned a master's degree in theater; Jennifer pursued a career in nursing. Rebecca went to Delhi and served as a missionary associate, helping to pioneer a new Project Rescue ministry in the brothels. During that time, God gave her a vision for rescuing and restoring the victims of trafficking through the arts.

God sent the young men our daughters would marry into our family. Tyler came to us through Chi Alpha, a ministry on scores of college and university campuses across America. He and Rebecca now live and work in Hyderabad with their two children, Judah and Ella.

Jonathan Barratt went to high school with Jennifer in Springfield, Missouri, before playing professional baseball in the minor league system of the Tampa Bay Devil Rays. He was advancing through the minors when physical challenges and injury abruptly ended his baseball career. Jon is blessed with an outstanding business mind. Today he leads the Project Rescue Foundation and brings an entrepreneurial spirit that is part and parcel of the greatest missionary outreaches. I have no doubt that Jon's skills qualify him to lead an organization much larger than ours.

Jennifer serves as our associate executive director. Her combination of executive ability—which absolutely does not come from me—and professional competence as a nurse make her an invaluable leader on our team. Jennifer served as the director of nursing in a senior living community where she gave oversight to 160 nursing staff members. She has her mother's gifts of diplomacy and grace, which are platinum gifts in the day-to-day environment of an office team.

The succession plan also includes Project Rescue offices in Europe, Africa, and Southern Asia. Dozens of young leaders, most from the nations where we have worked, lead this ministry. To be clear, Project Rescue is not a US ministry; it is a global ministry with an office in the US that resources the hundreds of dedicated team members who are in the trenches around the world.

One of our old friends recently visited our office in Springfield and commented that it was the only ministry he'd ever seen with four corner offices. That is the succession plan at Project Rescue, leaders serving together as a team here and around the world. When any of us move on, there is always someone there to step up.

None of us knows how long we have left. Both my parents and Beth's lived to a ripe old age. But one thing I know: none of us lives on this earth forever. Beth and I have a primary responsibility to steward the vision God gave us for the trafficked children of the world and to raise up leaders to rescue, restore, and equip them to every good work.

When I was a student at Southeastern more than fifty-five years ago, God told me, "I will break you into a million pieces, and I will feed you to a million children in India." He did everything He said He would do and more. And it has been a joy and delight. I absolutely know that I was born to give.

Project Rescue advisory board members, shown here meeting in Oxford, England, help us raise funds and develop strategies to support the young women and men God has helped us rescue and restore. More than fifty-one thousand women and men were ministered to in 2020 alone.

My daughter and son-in-law Rebecca and Tyler Shults lead our ministry in India. They are shown here with their children, Ella and Judah.

My daughter and son-in-law Jennifer and Jonathan Barratt lead the Project Rescue Foundation. They are shown here with their children, Gemma (left) and Madison.

165

ACKNOWLEDGMENTS

I T HAS BEEN a joy to share these stories of my life with you. This effort would not have been possible without the encouragement and support of my wife and life partner, Beth, who has been on this journey with me for forty-four years. She has been a resource, clarifier, editor, and thoughtful critic. I could not have done it without her.

I also want to thank our daughters, Rebecca and Jennifer, who have pushed me for years to write "the book." Rebecca spent hours of time interviewing me about every aspect of my life and work. Those hours of interviews provided source material. In her role as administrator for Project Rescue, Jennifer did her best to keep the problems off my desk for weeks on end so I could focus on completing this project. Their husbands, Tyler and Jon, have shown amazing patience as I've wandered down the back alleys of my memory and subjected them to long monologues over family dinners on a wide variety of topics.

My Indian colleagues have also made themselves available for hours of conversations about our work together. David Mohan, Ivan Satyavrata, and K. K. Devaraj have greatly enriched this effort with their comments and gentle corrections to my flawed recollections. John Higgins, David Stewart Sr., Kevin Donaldson, and Joe Gordon provided perspective on critical issues.

Our Project Rescue team in Springfield, Missouri, has been enormously helpful, as have our Project Rescue colleagues in Southern Asia and Europe. Their selfless dedication to rescuing and restoring the victims of sex trafficking has provided the inspiration for much of what we do. The stories I have told are their stories. None of them could have come to print without them.

For more than fifty years, I have been part of the Assemblies of God missionary family. Scores of colleagues, too numerous to mention, have been our partners in the great work of bringing the presence of God to peoples of Southern Asia. Many of these brothers and sisters are in heaven now. I am a debtor to their sacrifice and faithfulness. I am also indebted for the impact they made on my life.

I cannot conclude these acknowledgments without thanking my family—my brothers, Joel, Lem, and Tim, and my sister, Gloria—for their contributions to my life. There is also a vast universe of Grant, Hudson, and Buntin cousins. In the South, "cousinhood" is a secondary religion that binds us together. The cousins have contributed memories and family pictures. They were also my first "congregation."

I also want to thank the hundreds of churches, pastors, and friends who have sown prayers and finances into our ministry, in some cases for decades. Because of you we have always been "covered," especially in moments of crisis and trial.

Finally, I want to thank you for taking your time to read this book. It is my prayer that God has used it to challenge you to let Him break your life into a million pieces to feed the children of the world.

NOTES

CHAPTER 5

1. Winston Churchill, quoted in Ashton Applewhite, William R. Evans III, and Andrew Frothingham, *And I Quote* (New York: St. Martin's Press, 1992), 353.
2. George Otto Trevelyan, *The Life and Letters of Lord Macaulay*, vol. 1 (New York: Harper & Brothers, 1876), https://www.gutenberg.org/files/2647/2647-h/2647-h.htm.
3. Lorraine Boissoneault, "The Genocide the US Can't Remember, but Bangladesh Can't Forget," *Smithsonian*, December 16, 2016, https://www.smithsonianmag.com/history/genocide-us-cant-remember-bangladesh-cant-forget-180961490/.
4. "Mother Teresa of Calcutta," Weebly.com, accessed May 25, 2021, https://catholicsaintmotherteresa.weebly.com/pusue-of-social-justice.html.
5. "Mother Teresa of Calcutta," Weebly.com.
6. Kathryn Spink, *Mother Teresa: A Complete Authorized Biography* (New York: HarperCollins, 1997), 55.